No. of Copies	Grade Level	Code	Title	School Price	Total
_____	(Pre-Primer)	01201	**APPLE TREES**	$2.40	_____
_____		01202	Teacher's Edition	2.40	_____
_____	(Primer)	01203	**GINGERBREAD**	2.49	_____
_____		01204	Teacher's Edition	2.49	_____
_____	1	01205	**TOADSTOOLS**	3.15	_____
_____		01206	Teacher's Edition	3.15	_____
_____	2	01207	**ROLLER SKATES**	3.39	_____
_____		01208	Teacher's Edition	3.39	_____
_____	3	01209	**SAILBOATS**	3.69	_____
_____		01210	Teacher's Edition	3.69	_____
_____	4	01211	**WINDOWPANES**	4.11	_____
_____		01212	Teacher's Edition	4.11	_____
_____	5	01213	**FOX EYES**	4.32	_____
_____		01214	Teacher's Edition	4.32	_____
_____	6	01215	**SEABIRDS**	4.32	_____
_____		01216	Teacher's Edition	4.32	_____
_____	7	01217	**NORTHERN LIGHTS**	5.25	_____
_____		01218	Teacher's Edition	5.25	_____
_____	8	01219	**THUNDERBOLTS**	5.40	_____
_____		01220	Teacher's Edition	5.40	_____

Please send information on the following Field Reading Program:

Fold ☐ Kaleidoscope Readers   ☐ M___ Bay Mysteries

Tear along perforation

Helen Huus
Professor of Education
University of Missouri-Kansas City

Robert J. Whitehead
Professor of Education
Sacramento State College

Program Director
Henry A. Bamman
Professor of Education
Sacramento State College

Field Educational Publications, Incorporated

A Subsidiary of Field Enterprises, Incorporated
San Francisco   Addison, Ill.   Berkeley Heights, N.J.   Atlanta   Dallas

Apple Trees

Teacher's Edition

Field Literature Program

Acknowledgments

Rarely is a book the work of but one person; this book
is no exception. Among those who deserve special
thanks for their contributions are Miss Mary C. Renner,
Director of Audio-Visual Instruction, Upper Darby
Township Schools, Upper Darby, Pennsylvania, who
selected and reviewed the audio-visual aids
recommended in the Teacher's Guide; Miss Elizabeth
Breting, Librarian, and Mrs. Elizabeth Johnson,
Assistant Librarian, Children's Room, Plaza Branch
Library, Kansas City, Missouri, who were gracious and
helpful in locating books and making them available
for study.

Thanks are also due the many others who worked
behind the scenes and the publishers who consented to
the reprinting of text and illustrations from their
copyrighted works. Their contributions have permitted
the books in this program to reach a high level of literary
quality, and acknowledgment is made with gratitude
and appreciation.

CONTENTS

Introduction

PERSPECTIVE

It is not enough that young people *learn* to read. They must also *read.* Important effects of stimulating children to read and to continue reading are the self-satisfaction they feel in being able to read efficiently and the enjoyment they obtain from reading interesting stories, books, and poems. The key to all this is a knowledgeable teacher who appreciates both literature and young people.

Schools have spent a great deal of effort, time, and money in order to teach pupils how to read. But equal emphasis has not been given to fostering independent, personal reading so that young people turn to literature in pleasurable anticipation of enjoyment and knowledge.

In the past this neglect has been due to a lack of funds for libraries and librarians, to the inadequacy of the teacher's knowledge of books and the methodologies of teaching literature, and to the preoccupation with other school subjects. As a result, little or no time was devoted to the teaching of literature.

Now all this has changed. School districts are building and expanding elementary and junior high school libraries. Teachers are learning about books and methodologies for teaching young people about literature. As a result, time is being provided in the school program for the reading and enjoyment of good stories and poems and for learning what makes them literary.

For a number of reasons, teachers continue to need help in planning literature programs. First, it is difficult to select suitable materials for study from among the large numbers of books published annually. Second, it is a difficult task for the teacher to know which aspects of a poem or a story are worthy of study. Third, the teacher must make a judgment as to the difficulty both of concepts and of vocabulary in a series of stories at grade level before he can determine how much the readers can gain from the printed material. Finally, it is no small task to organize the available material into an orderly, sequential pattern of experiences for pupils.

Recognizing these needs of teachers, the authors of the Field Literature Program have made every effort to provide the means whereby the teacher can attain sound goals of instruction in literature.

PRINCIPLES UNDERLYING THE PROGRAM

Traditionally, basal reading programs in schools have been designed to teach students the skills of reading. Consequently, there has been little or insufficient emphasis on the ultimate goals of reading instruction: the acquisition of literary knowledge and the cultivation of a lifetime habit of critical, creative reading.

The Field Literature Program adheres to the concept that the basal reading program needs to be complemented by an enriching literature program in which students may practice and extend the skills acquired in the basal reading program. The Field Literature Program, which has been designed to implement this concept, is based upon certain fundamental principles regarding the value and place of the teaching of literature in the curriculum. These principles are:

1. Literary works are worthy of study for their own sake; that is, they serve as ends in themselves. However, such study will also result in the acquisition of knowledge, a growth in understanding of self and others, and an ever-increasing interest in the reading of literature.

2. The literary material chosen for study should be stimulating in content, should represent a variety of forms and styles of prose and poetry, and should be suited to a variety of purposes. The selections of which this series is composed include materials to match the different degrees of ability found within a school or class.

3. An appreciation of literature — that is, a sensitive recognition of its value and worth — comes from consistent exposure to writing of superior quality, whether by established authors or by contemporary writers.

4. An appreciation of literature is enhanced by a sound, sequentially organized program which incorporates reinforcement activities, such as (a) listening critically to a selection read aloud by a good reader, either teacher or student; (b) studying various aspects of literature in order to achieve better understanding and appreciation; (c) discussing the lives and works of authors and illustrators; and (d) sharing one's enjoyment of literature through discussion, writing, dramatization, art, music, and related expressive activities.

5. An appreciation of literature is dependent upon a ready supply of trade books, textbooks, and related visual aids. The close cooperation of teachers, librarians, administrators, and consultants is essential to the ultimate success of any literature program.

6. It is imperative that young readers study literature which pertains to their real interests and which deals with situations of genuine concern to them. The teacher should recognize the unique interests, needs, and abilities of each reader, and then build upon this framework in extending these interests to areas yet unknown to the reader. This dual approach is important for developing new interests.

7. The teacher holds a central position in developing in each young person a positive lifetime attitude toward literature. If the teacher

understands and appreciates the value of children's books, stories, and poems, has a genuine concern for the education of boys and girls, and is able to provide an exciting, functional program of literature, his students will be permanently enriched because of the experience.

8. Evaluation of the literature program must be made in terms of the personal development of each reader. Signs of growth will be reflected in his maturing interests, goals, and tastes in literature. The ultimate test of a program's success lies in the continuing reading of literature for pleasure throughout a lifetime.

OBJECTIVES OF THE PROGRAM

The Field Literature Program is planned to give students an ever-expanding understanding of literature — its contents, authors, genres, forms, and purposes. The objectives are applicable to each grade level from kindergarten to grade eight, but the depth of exploration and the emphases vary with the age and maturity of the students at the several levels. The differences, therefore, are those of degree rather than of kind. Thus, the Field Literature Program provides for continuing growth in literary knowledge from age level to age level, grade level to grade level, and maturity level to maturity level. Specifically, the objectives of the program are:

Objective 1: To create an appreciation and an understanding of what constitutes literature.

The enjoyment of literature is an important objective, for as students gain pleasure from reading, the experience will generate enthusiasm for future reading. One essential to such enjoyment is the acquisition of specific knowledge about the craftsmanship of the writer and the structural and content elements of literature.

There are many facets to the study of literary elements. The following list contains aspects of prose and poetry that are explored in the Field Literature Program:

a) Character development, as it unfolds through description, dialogue, and actions of the characters. Students are led to note the differences between static and growing characters.

b) Settings in time and place, as depicted by descriptions and illustrations.

c) Plot, as it involves the resolution of one or more internal or external conflicts. The plot is the significant pattern of action in the selection.

d) Theme, which provides unity and meaning to a literary work. A theme is the main idea on which a story is based. It often consists of a general truth about life or mankind, and it may be stated directly, as in a fable, or implied within a selection.

e) Genre, or type of literature, as it relates to the form and purpose of various selections. Genre refers to the characteristics that separate prose from poetry, fiction from nonfiction, and one form, such as the essay, from another form. Genre also relates to purpose; for example, selections can be categorized as narration, exposition, argument, or description.

f) Style, which includes (1) the language as it results from rhythm, rhyme, alliteration, and consonance in poetry, or from cadence and word order in dialogue and descriptive matter in prose; (2) the interpretation of ideas not directly stated, such as figures of speech (simile, metaphor, personification); symbolism; humor or satire; the relationship of cause and effect to character action; the prediction of events; the ability to follow sequence of idea or event and to consider relevance; and the determination of mood, tone, and atmosphere of a story or poem; and (3) an author's distinctive way of writing, his use of vocabulary, and his ability to strike a mood by employing humor, pathos, and other devices for his purpose.

It is not intended that pupils over-analyze a given selection. However, with repeated experience from story to story and from grade to grade, students should acquire a sound knowledge of what constitutes literature. They should also develop reasonable confidence in their own ability to recognize fine writing when they see it.

Objective 2: To acquaint students with their literary heritage.
Literature that has survived has done so because it has appealed to generation after generation. The eternal qualities and universal truths found in classical literature are as pertinent today as when the works were first written. It is important that today's generation also has the opportunity to become acquainted with those master-pieces that have survived and to note their contemporary relevance. In addition, an educated person is expected to have a familiarity with traditional literature, for allusions to it are found in contemporary journal articles, in advertising, and in daily conversation; art and music are based on traditional stories; and, best of all, the stories themselves are of enduring interest.

Objective 3: To foster a deep-rooted interest in and lasting enthusiasm for reading literature.
From the student's point of view, interest in the selections being read is the most important factor. For without reader interest, there can be no attention to the several facets of the work, no effort to attain a particular goal, and no realization of the lasting benefits to be derived from a lifetime habit of reading.

The collection and organization of the selections in the Field Literature Program were based upon studies of students' interests at different levels of maturity. These selections were chosen in order to provide material that would generate this interest and to expand the readers' horizons. However, careful selection and accurate placement of materials do not guarantee lasting interest on the part of young people. A student's interest in literature results from a blending of many factors. Appropriate presentation, readability, literary value, and attractive illustrations are among these factors; the reader's personal background of experiences is another vital element.

The Field Literature Program points out to young people that literature as a leisure-time activity is a focal point for enriching their lives. Books are to be enjoyed; for if there is no fun in reading and sharing literature, there can be little learning, little reaction, little relaxation, and little resolution of personal problems.

Objective 4: To help students foster their personal development and gain a fundamental understanding of the humanness of all people.

Literature helps readers know themselves. Through the Field Literature Program, the reader encounters worthwhile literary characters who lend comfort by grappling with and solving problems similar to the reader's own. Believable characters also provide models which aid young people in developing high ethical standards. Thus, each reader broadens his own experience and formulates a structure for resolving personal problems.

Similarly, the reader is afforded an opportunity to view people of other cultures, creeds, countries, and social levels. The student comes to appreciate the similarities between his own background and that of people elsewhere, both past and present, and to understand more fully than ever points of view other than his own. This gives him that sense of oneness, of belonging, and of security essential to mental and social adjustment.

Objective 5: To help students think critically and respond creatively in the world in which they live.

To children, reading literature is an adventure in discovery: discovery of characters worthy of emulation; of places, real and imaginary; of ideas worth examining; of language worth savoring. Most important, the reading of literature can aid the reader in a discovery of self in relation to others. A reader's examination of every facet of this adventure requires that he think through all aspects or components of the story or poem, and then draw conclusions based upon his personal values and his concept of what occurred in the selection he has been reading.

To help students articulate their response to the world in which they live, the following are supportive aims of the program:

a) To promote skills of communication. The variety and quality of the literary materials and exercises provide excellent opportunities for young people to sharpen their abilities to listen critically, to read aloud, and to speak — all so important in today's communication-oriented world. Several of the books at the early primary level contain a number of "listen to" selections, so that those children who cannot read for themselves can have the opportunity to hear and enjoy literature at their level.

b) To develop methods for expanding vocabulary and improving comprehension. Selections have been placed at appropriate grade levels in order to reflect increased vocabulary, comprehension, and growing concepts about literature, its qualities and characteristics, and concepts about the topics in the selection. The important concepts to be developed are highlighted in the Teacher's Guide and are made the bases for a variety of oral and written exercises.

Care was taken in measuring the appropriateness of all prose selections. With respect to vocabulary, the Dale-Chall Readability Formula was utilized to determine the placement of each selection above the primary grades, and to determine whether the selection would be rated core, easy, average, or advanced. Also considered were the interests, experiences, abilities, and purposes of the readers, along with the conceptual qualities of the selections. Definitions of words have been included to help explain difficult words and phrases, so that the literary excerpts can be used in their original form without adaptation.

c) To enhance and support the content fields. The Field Literature Program reinforces the regular study in the fields of mathematics, science, social studies, reading, language arts, and other areas. This is done by providing excerpts from animal and nature stories, historical fiction, biography, folk literature, space exploration, and the like. The stories, poems, and realistic accounts add meaningful detail, give life to fact, and function in colorful and dramatic fashion.

Although the Field Literature Program is not to be employed as a basal reading program, it is constructively supportive of reading comprehension and study skills and of vocabulary development. Specific teacher-directed activities are provided in the lessons of the Teacher's Guide in order to promote and encourage vocabulary development. Additionally, the selections incorporated in the Program are certainly meant for oral and silent reading and for practice in improving fluency and speed of reading, and they are supportive of the broad areas of the language arts — creative writing, dramatization, listening, and various aspects of oral communication.

MATERIALS

Only literature of the finest quality is to be found in the Field Literature Program. In order to insure maximum student interest and excellence in the choice of poems, stories, and selected excerpts, the following requirements were uppermost in the minds of the authors:

1. Selections should reflect the best writing of the best authors as judged by recognized experts and as reflected in authoritative published lists.
2. Selections should appeal to both boys and girls, though perhaps not always with equal interest in any given selection.
3. Selections of varying levels of difficulty should be provided for each grade to accommodate student variances in achievement and capability in reading.
4. Where feasible, original illustrations should be used, particularly in the primary-grade books. Exceptionally appropriate illustrations and an open, attractive format should be used throughout the series.
5. Taken as a whole, the excerpts should contain samples of structural elements of literature, exemplifying the aspects considered relevant for students in grades kindergarten through eight. Each book should build upon and extend the literary skills acquired in preceding books in the Program.
6. All prose and poetry should be presented in their original form, without alteration of vocabulary. Translated materials should remain faithful to the original.
7. A variety of literary types should be represented — prose and poetry, fiction and nonfiction, traditional and contemporary — with provision made for the inclusion of biography, autobiography, drama, essay, and other forms of literature.
8. Balance should be maintained in the choice of materials about cultures and social levels, both in the United States and abroad. There should be representative examples of literature by and about various minority groups. There should be a balance of material for children of both urban and rural areas.
9. The content of each text as a whole should develop positive attitudes in the student and contribute to his understanding of himself and others. The selections should stimulate intellectual growth, encourage emotional response, and develop awareness and sensitivity to the dignity of man and to the meaning and purpose in man's life in all places and at all times.

These requirements have been met in the preparation of the Field Literature Program.

ORGANIZATION: PRIMARY GRADES

The Field Literature Program is composed of ten pupils' books: a preprimer, a primer, a first reader, and one book each for grades two through eight. Post-reading activities are provided in each of the pupils' books. In addition, a Teacher's Guide accompanies each of the pupils' texts. It contains an introductory statement, a general teaching plan for the total program, a list of curriculum resources and audio-visual materials, and detailed lesson plans for all selections in the particular book. The pupils' books and the lesson plans in the Teacher's Guides are designed for flexibility of use by students and flexibility of instruction by teachers.

The prose and poetry selections in the pupils' texts at the preprimer and primer levels are organized into a unified whole rather than into units. The selections in these two books include many of the same types of themes found in the later books in the Field Literature Program. Young children are interested in the here and now and in their immediate environment, and the selections in the textbooks have been chosen with a recognition of these interests.

The textbooks for grades one, two, and three utilize the unit arrangement of six major strands or themes which link the books together. The unit plan is continued in later grades, but variations appropriate to the maturity level of the pupils have been made. The unit arrangement provides a continuity from grade to grade and a focus for the literary study within a grade. Many of the selections could be placed under more than one strand or theme, but judicious selection and placement allow important concepts to be developed and practical activities to be suggested.

The six major strands are as follows:

Adventure: real-life stories, poems, and plays about familiar people and places, past and present, as well as adventure stories and poems set in more distant lands.

Natural and physical science: fiction and nonfiction about wild and domesticated animals, exploration, conservation, and experimentation.

Around the world: literature about young people in other countries and cultures, past and present; the selections show the children at work, at school, and at play.

Folk literature: prose and poetry that exemplify the best of the tall tales, fables, chants, myths, legends, and hero tales appropriate to the particular grade level.

Fun and fantasy: humorous, nonsensical, imaginative, and make-believe stories and poems about animals and young people, both lifelike and fanciful, caught in surprising situations.

Interesting people: problem-probing selections that focus on believable characters from the past and the present who cope with genuine problems and concerns in familiar and unusual situations and settings.

In addition to the six major strands, the authors have chosen underlying themes that provide unity and focus for the reader. For example, the first unit in *Toadstools* deals generally with the major strand of adventure. More specifically, the selections share the common theme identified in the unit title "Surprises."

TEACHING SUGGESTIONS: PRIMARY GRADES

The Teacher's Guides for kindergarten through grade three include a teaching plan for every selection in each book—both prose selections and poems. Following is the general outline of the teaching plan for the selections:

PRE-READING PREPARATION

Gives a series of suggestions in three specific categories to aid the teacher in developing background, purpose, and motivation for the reading.

Background for the Selection

Supplies pertinent information about the author or gives a brief synopsis of the excerpt, or both. This section may also identify the central character, the setting, the style of writing, and the literary genre of the excerpt.

Elements of Literature

Provides background information about the literary elements to be explored by the teacher and the students. The elements listed in this section are developed in detail in the section "Interpreting Literature."

Introducing the Selection

Helps the reader establish purposes for reading, highlights the vocabulary important to the story, suggests activities to motivate the reading, and directs the student to read the selection silently or orally.

POST-READING EXTENSION

A series of activities designed to extend skills and interests. It contains three kinds of activities.

Exploring the Selection

Focuses upon an analysis of the content of each selection by having the readers react orally or in writing to the questions following each selection in the Sharing Time portions of the text. Additional questions are provided in the teaching plan to focus on main ideas and details encountered in the selection. Factual questions are included to assure literal comprehension; thought questions, to help the children read critically and creatively; and application questions, to relate the concepts to the children's lives and actions.

Interpreting Literature

Provides commentary, questions, and study activities related to the aspects of literature enumerated in the section "Elements of Literature." This section employs the standard terminology of literary discussion, with the terms introduced at the appropriate grade level.

Developing Language Skills

Emphasizes learning and creative activities. This section includes exercises in vocabulary development, interpretive and research writing programs, and suggested activities in story-telling, art, choral reading, dramatization, handicrafts, and music. Learnings are further enriched through recommendations for independent reading and through examination of films, filmstrips, recordings, and tapes.

PACING: PRIMARY GRADES

The selections within each book are suitable for introduction to the class or group. Because children in the primary grades learn to read at different ages, the class will include some children who can read and some who cannot. The teaching plans have provided for this situation, and pupils can gain reading readiness, information, and pleasure from following along in their books as others read and from browsing in the picture books listed as supplementary.

There is no one best way to schedule time for the use of the Field Literature Program. A teacher may wish to use one of several plans at different times during the year:

1. Daily allocation of 20 or 30 minutes to the Program.
2. Twice-a-week periods of an hour each for the Program. In this plan, developmental reading is taught Monday through Wednesday or Monday, Wednesday, and Friday, with the Field Literature Program being used on Thursday and Friday in the first instance or on Tuesday and Thursday in the second.
3. Informally scheduled program, with children reading when opportunities arise before and during the school day. At least one formal weekly time period should be included in the schedule if this procedure is used.

The amount of time devoted to literature will be dependent upon the characteristics of the students served and upon the grade level. In kindergarten, the teacher reads aloud the selection in the text and utilizes the supplementary books. A period of 10 to 15 minutes is often long enough for kindergarten and first grade, depending on the attention span of the children and their background with books. In the first grade, the teacher will read aloud some of the selections, and other selections will be read by the pupils themselves as they become capable. In second and third grades, pupils can spend

20 minutes reading their own textbooks. They might also be given additional time for reading independently as they become more and more competent.

A teacher might elect to spend two or three weeks on each unit and complete the anthology in one semester, leaving the second semester for individual reading of stories suggested in the bibliographies in the Teacher's Guide. Or he might pace the course so that students complete a unit, then read widely before going on to the next unit. This plan has the advantage of providing a common jumping-off spot for group and class discussions, since students are reading a common theme. There is no particular advantage in speedily going through the reading without stopping to savor the literary aspects; nor is there an advantage in moving so slowly that the class gets bored reading one topic. However, since these stories and poems are of so high a quality that they bear rereading, pupils should be encouraged to reread enough to become thoroughly familiar with the selections.

EVALUATION

Evaluation of a program in literature is concerned with examining the student's appreciation and enjoyment of what he has read. Changes in tastes, goals, and attitudes as a result of the experiences with literature are important objectives of the Field Literature Program. Important, too, is the acquaintance with the literary heritage, for it forms a vital part in cultural growth.

Evaluation is effective to the extent that it is planned, understood, and used in concert by the teacher and the students. Evaluating and judging the development of individuals on the basis of such intangibles as appreciation and enjoyment is not an easy task, but it can be implemented by a consideration of the following points:

1. The frequency with which free time, in and out of class, is used to read for fun and relaxation.
2. The quality and, to a lesser extent, the quantity of literature being read.
3. The achievement of a broader knowledge of the structure of literature — its themes, plots, characters, forms, genres, vocabulary.
4. The eagerness with which well-liked stories and poems are shared through oral, written, dramatic, or artistic modes of communication.
5. The extension of an individual's interest in a special area of literature.
6. The acquisition of an understanding of different people of different eras, cultures, and countries, but especially the attainment of a better understanding of self.
7. The movement along the pathway toward a lifetime habit of reading literature.

RESOURCES

The following list of films and books is a selected compilation of materials related only to the methodologies of teaching various aspects of literature. A brief annotation follows each reference.

Films

Let's Try Choral Reading. 11-minute black-and-white film. McGraw-Hill Films. Explains and demonstrates the values of choral reading.

Literature Appreciation—How To Read Biographies. 14-minute color and black-and-white film. Coronet Films. Writings about Washington and Lincoln are used to show how biography helps the reader understand history.

Literature Appreciation—How To Read Novels. 14-minute color and black-and-white film. Coronet Films. Encourages students to find out about the author, to study characterization, and to visualize the setting and the action of the story.

Literature Appreciation—How To Read Plays. 14-minute color and black-and-white film. Coronet Films. Reconstruction of a stage production enables the reader to grasp the visual, oral, and dramatic content of a play.

Literature Appreciation—How To Read Poetry. 11-minute color and black-and-white film. Coronet Films. How to increase the pleasure of reading poetry through understanding the poet and recognizing word devices that convey poetic ideas.

Literature Appreciation—Stories. 14-minute color and black-and-white film. Coronet Films. Illustrated are ways to appreciate stories through a study of plot, character, setting, and style of writing.

Lively Art of Picture Books. 57-minute color film. Weston Woods Studios. Explores what makes a good picture book through interviews with Barbara Cooney, Robert McCloskey, and Maurice Sendak. Works of 36 illustrators are shown.

Poems Are Fun. 11-minute color and black-and-white film. Coronet Films. A class discovers poetry, choral speaking, and the fun of writing verse.

Poetry for Beginners. 11-minute color and black-and-white film. Coronet Films. A second-grade boy writes poems about things he thinks, sees, and feels.

Reading for Pleasure. 11-minute color and black-and-white film. Coronet Films. Describes the ways in which books can give pleasure.

Stories Should Be Shared. 15-minute color film. Wayne State University. Elementary school children act out a group of stories they have read.

Story Acting Is Fun. 11-minute color and black-and-white film. Coronet Films. How to act out experiences, poems, and stories.

The Story of a Book. 11-minute color film. Churchill Films. Holling C. Holling and his wife explain the process of doing the research for and writing their book *Pagoo, the Story of a Hermit Crab.*

Storytelling: Can You Tell It in Order? 11-minute black-and-white film. Coronet Films. Shows how events in sequence make sense and relates this concept to good storytelling.

Telling Stories to Children. 27-minute color film. University of Michigan. Discusses and demonstrates the theoretical and practical techniques of storytelling.

What Is Poetry. 10-minute color film. Bailey-Film Associates. Compares and contrasts a journalistic style of writing and a poem.

What's in a Play. 17-minute color film. Bailey-Film Associates. Analyzes and illustrates dramatic action.

What's in a Story. 14-minute color and black-and-white film. Bailey-Film Associates. Indicates what a story tells through its plot and characters.

Recordings

The Nature of Poetry. Recording. Spoken Arts. Artist Frank Baxter talks about poetry.

Ruth Sawyer, Storyteller. Recording. Weston Woods Studios. Ruth Sawyer discusses and demonstrates the fine points of storytelling.

Directory for Audio-Visual Aids

Bailey-Film Associates, 11559 Santa Monica Boulevard, Los Angeles, California 90025

Churchill Films, 662 North Robertson Boulevard, Los Angeles, California 90069

Coronet Films, 65 East South Water Street, Chicago, Illinois 60601

Eye Gate House, Inc., 146–01 Archer Avenue, Jamaica, New York 11435

Jam Handy School Service, 2821 East Grand Boulevard, Detroit, Michigan 48211

McGraw-Hill Films, 330 West 42nd Street, New York, New York 10018

National Film Board of Canada, 680 Fifth Avenue, New York, New York 10019

Society for Visual Education, Inc., 1345 West Diversey Parkway, Chicago, Illinois 60614

Spoken Arts Recordings, Encyclopaedia Britannica Educational Corporation, 425 North Michigan Avenue, Chicago, Illinois 60611

Sterling Educational Films, P.O. Box 8497, Universal City, Los Angeles, California 91608

University of Michigan, Audio-Visual Educational Center, 416 Fourth Street, Ann Arbor, Michigan 48103

Wayne State University, Audio Visual Productions Center, 680 Putnam, Detroit, Michigan 48202

Weston Woods Studios, Weston, Connecticut 06880

Books

Anderson, Paul S., and Irene S. Francis. *Storytelling with the Flannelboard.* Minneapolis: T. S. Denison & Co., Inc., 1963. Tips on technique.

Applegate, Mauree. *When the Teacher Says, "Write a Poem."* New York: Harper & Row, 1965. Good ideas on how to motivate children to write creatively. Companion volume: *When the Teacher Says, "Write a Story."*

Arbuthnot, May Hill. *Children and Books*. Chicago: Scott, Foresman & Co., 1964. A textbook on children's literature; strong in methods of teaching all aspects of poetry.

Armstrong, Chloe, and Paul Brandes. *The Oral Interpretation of Literature*. New York: McGraw-Hill Book Co., 1963.

Bamman, Henry, et al. *Oral Interpretation of Children's Literature*. Dubuque, Iowa: William C. Brown Co., 1970. On reading aloud, poetry, choral speaking, and storytelling.

Bromberg, Murray. *Making Literature Lessons Live: A Practical Guide to Success in the Teaching of Literature*. Englewood Cliffs, N.J.: Prentice-Hall, Inc., 1961. A booklet on planning literature programs.

Carlson, Ruth K. *Sparkling Words: Two Hundred Practical and Creative Writing Ideas*. Champaign, Illinois: National Council of Teachers of English, 1965.

Christensen, Fred B., and Hope M. Scrogin. *Recipes for Creative Writing*. Santa Fe Springs, California: Creative Teaching Press, Inc., n.d. Over one hundred 4-by-6 cards to stimulate children to write creatively.

A Curriculum for English, Grades 1–6. Lincoln, Nebraska: University of Nebraska Press, 1966. A six-book outline program for the teaching of literature, with additional books on poetry and linguistics.

Dunning, Stephen. *Teaching Literature to Adolescents: Poetry*. Chicago: Scott, Foresman & Co., 1966. A paperback methods book.

Films for Children. New York: Educational Film Library Association, 1965. Annotated list of 272 films for literature classes.

Fitzgerald, Burdette. *World Tales for Creative Dramatics and Storytelling*. Englewood Cliffs, N.J.: Prentice-Hall, Inc., 1962.

Howes, Alan. *Teaching Literature to Adolescents: Plays*. Chicago: Scott, Foresman & Co., 1967. Companion to the Dunning book and others.

Huck, Charlotte, and Doris Young Kuhn. *Children's Literature in the Elementary School*. New York: Holt, Rinehart & Winston, 1968. A college text, with Part 3 devoted to developing literature programs.

Jacobs, Leland B., editor. *Using Literature with Young Children*. New York: Teachers College Press, Columbia University, 1965. Booklet covering 12 aspects of methodology.

Kase, Robert. *Stories for Creative Acting*. New York: Samuel French, 1961.

Loban, Walter, Margaret Ryan, and James R. Squire. *Teaching Language and Literature, Grades 7–12*. New York: Harcourt Brace Jovanovich, Inc., 1961. Part 3 deals with methods of teaching literature.

Meeker, Alice M. *Enjoying Literature with Children*. New York: Odyssey Press, Inc., 1969. General methodologies are considered in this paperback.

Moore, Vardine. *Pre-School Story Hour*. Metuchen, N.J.: Scarecrow Press, 1966. Many ideas on how to use literature.

Petty, Walter T., and Mary E. Bowen. *Slithery Snakes and Other Aids to Children's Writing*. New York: Appleton-Century-Crofts, 1967. Ways to motivate young people to write.

Rasmussen, Margaret, editor. *Literature with Children*. Washington, D.C.: Association for Childhood Education, 1961. Pamphlet on 12 aspects of literature methods.

Reasoner, Charles F. *Releasing Children to Literature*. New York: Dell Publishing Company, Inc., 1968. Aids for introducing children to literature.

Sawyer, Ruth. *The Way of the Storyteller*. New York: Viking Press, 1962. History, philosophy, and approach to storytelling are presented along with 11 of the author's favorite stories.

Schreiber, Morris, et al. *An Annotated List of Recordings in the Language Arts*. Champaign, Illinois: National Council of Teachers of English, 1964.

Siks, Geraldine B. *Children's Literature for Dramatization: An Anthology*. New York: Harper & Row, 1964. Stories to act out and tell.

Smith, James A. *Creative Teaching of Reading and Literature in the Elementary School*. Boston: Allyn & Bacon, 1967. Helps build appreciations and standards.

Wagner, Joseph, and Robert Smith. *Teacher's Guide to Storytelling*. Dubuque, Iowa: William C. Brown Co., 1958. Includes material on flannelboards and puppetry.

Walter, Nina W. *Let Them Write Poetry*. New York: Holt, Rinehart & Winston, 1962. A book about the teaching of poetry appreciation through the writing of poetry.

Whitehead, Robert J. *Children's Literature: Strategies of Teaching*. Englewood Cliffs, N.J.: Prentice-Hall, 1968. A book about various aspects of methodology.

The Preprimer, which is the first book in the Field Literature Program, serves as the child's introduction to a planned program of study. The literature represents some of the best material written for children. It is important that a child's first experiences with books in school be pleasant and rewarding. The intent of this program is to provide just such experiences and to make literature an integral part of the child's day, both in and out of school.

Content. Books for young children cater to their interests and needs. Children who are just beginning school have had time and opportunity for only limited experiences, which places certain restrictions on the types and topics of books suitable for or interesting to them.

This book is composed of fifteen selections — four stories and eleven poems. The stories differ from each other in type; two are realistic, one is fanciful, and one is a folktale. Rather than emphasize plot, the authors of the realistic stories present a number of incidents or examples related to the main theme of the story.

The original versions of the selections have been used without adaptation of vocabulary. Only one selection has been abridged in order to make it short enough for classroom use. In many instances the art in the original books has also been obtained, so that the child's introduction to these selections gives him the added experience of seeing illustrations that form a part of the literary masterpieces themselves.

Organization. The selections in this book are organized not by units but by logical and psychological appropriateness. You will note that the types and subjects of the selections relate to children's interest and comprehension levels, and that the book as a whole possesses an artistic integrity of its own.

The Teaching Plans. The plans for teaching each selection in the text follow the general pattern described in the Introduction to the Program. Each lesson plan includes the Pre-Reading Preparation and Post-Reading Extension for using the text material. Supplementary books, poems, and audio-visual aids are suggested to complement the lesson. You may also wish to add your own choices.

The experience of literature is a combination of language, idea, and emotion. For this reason, hearing a story read or told, when the sounds of the language can make their contribution, gives an added dimension to the work itself. An additional value is gained from the physical presence of another — the reader or storyteller — who can share the sorrows and joys of the selection and bring all the listeners into the charmed story circle.

The plans for this book assume that you will read these stories and poems aloud to the children as a group. Because of variations in children's backgrounds, concepts that could cause difficulty are explained in the lesson plans. The questions asked children in both the pupils' text and in the teaching plans vary in difficulty in order to provide for individual differences in level of ability. Should you have in your group or class a child who already reads well, you could let him read on occasion; but since this is a literature rather than a reading program, there is merit in having you present the material yourself.

Because few pupils learn from a single exposure to an idea, you should read and reread these selections to the class whenever there is an opportunity to do so. Pupils can easily learn the poems just by hearing them repeated often, rather than by sitting down to memorize them. Take advantage of odd moments during the day to say a poem with the children and, as their repertoire increases, develop little on-the-spot programs in which one group presents the poems and the other pupils become the audience. Should you have visitors, such as parents or the school principal or a supervisor, let them have a chance to share the fun.

The audio-visual aids suggested in connection with most of the lessons will extend the visual and auditory experiences of the children. Should you have difficulty obtaining the materials for the time you wish to use them, simply use them when they do come and review the story or poem at the same time. This is one of the charms of literature—the best writing bears repetition gracefully and, instead of becoming worn, seems to gain luster with use.

Not all the possible elements of literary quality are discussed in detail in the lesson plans, but only those considered especially noteworthy in each selection. In addition, every effort has been made to provide a balanced representation of literary elements suitable for the pupils. It is important that you note the literary elements and incorporate them in your teaching, for merely reading a story provides but a superficial exposure. By giving depth and emphasis to a selection, you will help your pupils think about ideas they would otherwise ignore or fail to recognize.

The suggestions for each story are too numerous to be completed in one day's lesson; therefore, use your judgment on where to "break" the lesson. You can return to the selections again and again and use the ideas you omitted before. Do add your own experiences and creative ideas in using these plans, for, after all, the *art* of teaching resides in the individual teacher's use of the suggestions and materials she has available.

So, as you approach this book, do so with an open mind and a light heart. Good reading to you and the class!

In presenting the Preprimer to the children, let them have a chance to browse through the book and enjoy the pictures. Some teachers object to this practice, because they believe it takes the surprise out of the lesson when children have already seen the pictures. However, the selections included in the book bear repeated use, and the pictures can be looked at again and again until they become familiar to the pupils. Children enjoy the security of the known, and they like to hear stories and poems they recognize. You are likely to tire of the material much sooner than they!

Introducing the Book

1. Announce to the class that you have a very special surprise for them. First let them guess; then tell them the surprise is a beautiful new book, full of stories and poems.
2. Before you give each child his book, ask the children what they know about using books. This should lead to a discussion of the need for clean hands, careful handling, and so on. You might later make a chart entitled "Using Books."
3. Tell the children that as soon as they get their books they can look through them for a few minutes just for fun. Then select enough children to help pass out the books. Give pupils enough time to browse through the books so they seem satisfied for the present.

Examining the Book

1. After you have allowed the children a chance to browse, encourage them to give spontaneous reactions. Then call attention to the title of the book on the front cover and explore what it suggests to them. Make sure that pupils understand the meaning of the word *title*.
2. Show children how to hold a book properly, or have a child who is doing it right show the class. (This entails holding the book on the center spine at the bottom of the book, using one hand and leaving the other hand free to turn the pages. If children need both hands to hold the book, they will have to put it on the desk or in their laps when they wish to turn a page.) Have the pupils practice holding the book and turning pages without wetting their fingers.
3. Hold up your book to show the title page and ask the children to find that page. (This will show how well they can match format.) Some may have difficulty, and if they do, help them find the page

by showing them the pages to turn until they come to the title page. Discuss with them what is on this page and the facing page: the title, the author, and the company that published the book. Then turn to the Contents and do the same. Note the page numbers for each story and see if children can read any of the numbers. (Few can at this stage of their learning.) You might put one of the numbers on the chalkboard and find out whether anyone can match it with the same number on the Contents page.

4. Tell the names of some of the selections and let the children suggest what the stories and poems might be about. A few children may know some of the selections already, so tell them they will have an opportunity to enjoy the stories and poems again.

5. Point out that at the end of some of the stories there are pages with questions for pupils to answer. Explain that each of these pages has the title "Sharing Time," and that the questions will enable each child to share what he has learned about the selection. Show them the Sharing Time page for "Hey Diddle Diddle," the first selection in the book. Help them find the page by matching, and then call attention to the question marks at the end of each question.

Discussing the Contents of the Book

1. Point out that some stories in the book are about real things that could happen. Let the children name some things they could really do, like swinging, playing in the little house, looking at TV, etc. Then say that some stories are make-believe, or pretend, and let the children think of "pretend" things. (Encourage ideas of being huge or very small, and of talking animals or objects, but remember that at this age the line between fact and fancy is very thin.)

2. Tell the children that some of the stories in the book are so old that their grandmothers and grandfathers knew them when they were boys and girls and that some of the poems are even older than that. Let them find some pictures they consider old-fashioned. Then tell them that some stories and poems are very new and let them find pictures that give them this idea. (They may have difficulty in deciding, but do not be too concerned.)

3. End the discussion by letting the pupils react to the book as a whole, making any comments they wish. Then tell the pupils that they will have many opportunities to see the book again and to enjoy the good stories and poems it contains.

Hey Diddle Diddle

PAGES 9–13

PRE-READING PREPARATION

Background for the Selection

This selection is taken from *The Hey Diddle Diddle Picture Book* illustrated by Randolph Caldecott. (The Caldecott Award, which is given annually for the best-illustrated children's book, is named for him.) "Hey Diddle Diddle" is a favorite Mother Goose rhyme that is nearly two hundred years old.

The illustrations for this rhyme are among Caldecott's best, for he captures the humor and action of the characters with his expressive lines and detailed interpretation. These qualities are shown, for example, in the expression on the faces of the two pigs, and the glimpse of the room as the dish and the spoon run away. Caldecott lived from 1846 to 1886; though this book was published in the 1870's, the illustrations are as appropriate today as they were then.

Since many characters and situations in Mother Goose are foreign to today's children, illustrations are necessary to help them obtain the images and concepts inherent in the verses. Illustrations have thus become an integral aspect of the traditional rhymes, and Caldecott's illustrations have become classic.

Elements of Literature

Mother Goose rhymes have been popular with generations of children. The rhymes contain the same elements of appeal that are found in other types of poetry. "Hey Diddle Diddle" appeals to children principally because the imaginative idea is presented through humorous action and the use of nonsense words, complemented by the illustrations. The following aspects are therefore emphasized in this lesson:

1. the humor of the situation.
2. the use of nonsense words.
3. the excellent illustrations.

Introducing the Selection

1. Tell the children that the first selection in their books is a Mother Goose rhyme. Ask the children to name any Mother Goose rhymes

they know and let a few children recite some of the rhymes. If a child recites "Hey Diddle Diddle," just accept it at this point, for you will come back to it later.

2. Ask the children what they know about cows—where they live, what they can do. Some children may never have seen a real cow; so let those who have seen cows tell what they look like, how big they are, what color they are, and so on. Emphasize the placid, contented nature of cows, because the contrast of the cow's action in the verse is one element of its humor.

3. Tell the children that the rhyme in their books is a funny one and that they will find several things in it that they will enjoy and can talk about later.

4. Direct the children to open their books to the first story on page 9. You may wish to write the number on the chalkboard for children to match. If children have difficulty in finding the page, let them help each other, or help them yourself.

5. When everyone has the right page, ask them to look at the illustration on the facing page. Let the children find the pigs, cow, chickens, dog, and bird; let them talk about what they think the animals are doing and where they live.

6. Then turn their attention to page 9 and ask what they think the cat is <u>about to do</u>. *has just done?* (Play the violin.) Ask them to listen as you read the page, and have them turn the pages as you direct.

7. Read the rest of the rhyme, and exaggerate the turning of your pages so the children can do the same. In this way they will have the proper picture before them as you read the text.

POST-READING EXTENSION

Exploring the Selection

Sharing Time

After you finish reading the selection, turn your attention to page 13, which contains the Sharing Time activities. Read each one aloud, but identify each by number as you do so.

The following are answers to the Sharing Time questions:

1. Some literal-minded children will answer "to see such fun," but pursue the question until the elements of the cat fiddling and the cow jumping over the moon are brought out.

2. Answers will vary, but accept any response that is in keeping with the spirit of the rhyme and the picture. The picture on page 12 might suggest an elopement. Some children, who note the picture on the Sharing Time page, may say that the dish and spoon went off to sit together.

3. Answers will vary, but see if the child can figure out why the part is funny to him.

4. Children may say "Dance" or "Keep time to the music with your

foot,'' or a similar answer. The idea of music stimulating action ought to be expressed.

Call attention to the picture on page 10, showing the cow jumping over the moon. Ask these questions:

8/10 Know about

1. Do you think a cow really can jump over the moon? (Those who remember the astronauts in the summer of 1969 may have factual information to back up their answers.)
2. Who might the person in this picture be? (The concept of a milkmaid may be new to the children, but they may figure out that it is a person whose pail of milk has been thrown into the air by the cow's leap.)
3. What do you think made the cow jump over the moon? (The children may connect this action with the cat's fiddling so well that it makes even cows want to dance and leap.)

Interpreting Literature

Humor

1. This Mother Goose rhyme is humorous and fanciful. The humor is based on a ludicrous situation which includes a cat that fiddles, a cow that jumps, a dog that laughs, and a dish and spoon that run away. The basis for the humor is that everyday animals and objects are behaving in ways that are not natural. Have children point out the fanciful, humorous actions of the animals.

Nonsense words

2. The use of nonsense words is typical of Mother Goose rhymes and other humorous poetry. The words *hey, diddle, diddle* have the additional advantage of being fun to say. As the *diddle diddle's* are rolled off, the child is amused by the way his tongue behaves. Let the children say *hey, diddle, diddle* several times.

Illustrations

3. This "Hey Diddle Diddle" rhyme is taken from a picture book, and like all books of this type, the pictures are an integral part of the story. The illustrations by Caldecott give a very realistic and extremely amusing interpretation of the action in the rhyme. For example, the illustration facing page 9 shows the farmyard animals cavorting around. Have children note the two friendly pigs, with their arms (forelegs) entwined as they gaily march. Note also the attitude of the cow as she skips along behind. Call attention to the children in the illustration on page 9. Ask if these children are living today and find out why the pupils think they are not. (Their clothes are different.) Let pupils guess why the children may be dressed up and where they are going. In the picture on page 10, note the clever, realistic way in which the cow is jumping over the moon. Finally, in the picture on page 12, note the graceful, dancing figures, the other "dish" people, and the long strides of the runaways.

Developing Language Skills

Vocabulary development

1. Children might recognize a *fiddle* from the pictures, but they may be unfamiliar with the word. Ask them if they know another

name for the instrument the cat is playing. They will probably say *violin*. If you have other pictures of violins, show these to the children.

The names of farm animals can be reviewed (*cow*, *pig*, *hens*, or *chickens*); and if the class is rather knowledgeable, let them tell about these animals.

Those who have already heard the "Hey Diddle Diddle" rhyme might know the version that goes, "The little dog laughed to see such *sport*" rather than "to see such *fun.*" Ask the children if the two words mean the same thing and get them to see that *sport* is a kind of *fun*, while *fun* might also include other things besides *sport.*

Interpretive activities 2. See if children can now say the rhyme from memory. Many of them will be able to do so; others can if they follow the pictures in the book. Let several different children try, then have all the children say the rhyme in unison.

Have children draw their own illustrations for the rhyme, then place all the pictures on a bulletin board with the title and rhyme printed on tagboard. (Some schools have a hall display case that might also be used.)

Research activities 3. Ask the children to note the way in which the cow jumps over the moon in the Caldecott picture. Bring in other versions and let the children compare those pictures of the cow with Caldecott's. (Tasha Tudor's illustration is similar to Caldecott's.)

Books to read 4. Have available a copy of *The Hey Diddle Diddle Picture Book* by Randolph Caldecott. Children will be interested in all the pictures illustrating the rhyme. Have other Mother Goose books for the children to see, such as Blanche Fisher Wright's *Real Mother Goose*, *Ring O' Roses* by L. Leslie Brooke, *Mother Goose* by Tasha Tudor, and Marguerite de Angeli's *Book of Nursery and Mother Goose Rhymes.*

Audio-visual aids 5. The following audio-visual aid is recommended for use with this selection:
Hey Diddle Diddle and Baby Bunting, The Milkmaid. Color and sound filmstrip. Weston Woods Studios. Includes the Caldecott sketches.

Who Likes the Rain?

PAGE 14

PRE-READING PREPARATION

Background for the Selection

This simple, four-line poem is a good one to use with young children, because it contains good literary elements as well as a single, understandable idea. The poet, Clara Doty Bates, captures a child's-eye view of the duck who, like the child perhaps, "likes the rain." The "three-toed track" is obviously made by the toes of the duck's feet. Duck feet have webs between the toes, which serve as paddles for swimming. If you are not too familiar with ducks, you might like to know that their feathers are made waterproof by the duck's natural oils.

Elements of Literature

Children like poetry because it has rhythm, sound, and idea. Although the accent, or meter, of this poem is not so pronounced as in some others, two elements are well exemplified:

1. the unique idea expressed by a figure of speech.
2. the sounds of the words.

Introducing the Selection

1. Ask the children what they like best to do on a rainy day. If they seem reticent, suggest some outdoor activities like walking under an umbrella and listening to the plop of the raindrops; or hearing their rubbers squish in the mud and splash on the sidewalks; or running around in a bathing suit during a warm summer rain and splashing in the puddles.
2. Let children who do not like the rain tell why they feel that way. They may mention the loud claps of thunder and the surprising flashes of lightning, the fact that they need to stay indoors, and the darkness in the middle of the day that is unusual and therefore may be upsetting.
3. Then ask the children when they like to be out in the rain. Try to elicit from them the fact that rain can be fun if one is properly dressed for it. This could lead to a discussion of rainwear of different types: plastic, rubber, oilskin, treated fabrics, leather, and

31

the like. You might also ask children if they know how different pets react to rain.

4. Read the title of the poem and ask children to guess who it might be that likes the rain. Let several children try to answer. Do not be dismayed if someone who remembers the picture from having looked ahead answers correctly at this point. Have the pupils open their books and look at the picture. (You can write the page number on the chalkboard for children to match.)

5. Ask pupils to listen, as you read the poem, to see why the duck likes the rain.

POST-READING EXTENSION

Exploring the Selection

Questions to ask

1. Ask the children why the duck likes the rain. (He has red rubbers on.)

2. Pursue the point as to why one might like the rain when he is wearing waterproof footwear. (Few pupils like to *stay* wet, even though they may not mind *getting* wet.) Relate this idea to the children's getting wet feet and sitting in school all day. Ask the children how they dress for rainy weather and how they protect their schoolbooks, for example, in the rain.

3. Discuss other waterproof qualities of the duck, such as his feathers. Show pictures to supplement those in the textbook, for some children may be unfamiliar with ducks. Point out the duck's red, webbed feet..

Interpreting Literature

Figure of speech

1. Poems say things in a different way from prose; they often do this through vivid images and ideas. One of these images is presented by the *metaphor*. The metaphor is an implied comparison between two different things. It is a figure of speech in which a word or phrase that ordinarily means one thing is used about another thing in order to suggest a likeness between the two. The metaphor implies a likeness, whereas a simile says specifically that one is like the other by use of the words *like* or *as*.

   In this poem, the metaphor of the duck feet having "red rubbers on" is the point to note. It is, of course, inappropriate to use the word *metaphor* with children of this age, but the idea expressed by the duck's red-rubbered, waterproof feet can be noted. Ask pupils why the poem says the duck has "red rubbers" on. You might refer the children to the illustration of the duck.

Rhyme

2. Call attention to the words that "sound alike at the end"—*track* and *quack*. Children may think of other rhyming words such as *black*, *back*, *tack*, *sack*, *Jack*, *rack*, and *pack*.

Developing Language Skills

1. Two words in the poem that will need explaining are:

cunning: pretty and dear; attractive
three-toed track: a track made by three toes

Children might try drawing a three-toed track on the chalkboard.

2. Reread the poem and ask children to be the ducks and say the "quacks." Then let them try to say the entire poem with you. You might next let a group ask the question in the title and have another group answer by reading the poem. Perhaps individual children will then volunteer to say the whole poem. Later, let children illustrate the poem and mount their pictures on the bulletin board.

The poem reprinted in the pupil's text is actually the first stanza of a longer poem by Clara Doty Bates. You may wish to read and discuss the remaining stanzas with the children:

"I," cried the dandelion, "I."
"My roots are thirsty, my buds are dry."
And she lifted her little yellow head
Out of her green and grassy bed.

"I hope 'twill pour! I hope 'twill pour!"
Croaked the tree toad at his gray bark door.
"For with a broad leaf for a roof
I am perfectly weather-proof."

Sang the brook, "I welcome every drop;
Come, come dear rain drops, never stop
Till a great river you make of me,
Then I will carry you to the sea."

Children might know and like to say the old rhyme:

Rain, rain go away.
Come again another day.
Little _____ wants to play.

They can substitute whichever name they wish in the space.

3. Ask children to find out what else they can about ducks. When they do, give them a chance to tell about their findings.

4. Have *Real Mother Goose*, by Blanche Fisher Wright, or some other Mother Goose book available in order to read other rain poems like "One Misty, Moisty Morning" and "Doctor Foster Went to Gloucester." You might also get a copy of *A Child's Garden of Verses* by Robert Louis Stevenson, and read his four-line poem, "Rain." Also try to get *Umbrella* by Taro Yashima, for the pictures are exceptionally lovely.

Audio-visual aids 5. The following audio-visual aids are recommended for use with this selection:

Rain Drop Splash. Color and sound filmstrip. Weston Woods Studios. Shows how raindrops finally reach the sea.

It's Raining! It's Pouring! in the set *A Child's World of Poetry—Group 1.* Record and color study print. Society for Visual Education, Inc. Includes several other rain poems.

Wind and Rain, in the *Listening, Looking, Feeling* series. Color and sound filmstrip. Bailey–Film Associates. Just rain and the way it looks and sounds.

Firefly

PAGE 15

PRE-READING PREPARATION

Background for the Selection

This poem is included in Elizabeth Madox Roberts' book of poetry for children, *Under the Tree*. She was a gifted writer who could see the world from a child's point of view and could capture his wonder and amazement in simple, direct language. This quality has made her poetry appealing to adults and children alike. Her poem "Firefly" captures the child's awe at seeing a firefly, or lightning bug, and realizing that it is a flying light—"a little light with wings."

Elements of Literature

One characteristic of poetry is its terseness, its amazing compression of ideas into a few words so that the reader gains concepts and impressions equal or superior to those gained from longer selections in prose. When the idea of a poem is conveyed with an intensity of feeling, the reader reacts both emotionally and intellectually. Since this poem exemplifies both of these characteristics, the following points will be discussed:
   1. the simplicity with which the idea is stated and repeated.
   2. the mood created by the poem.

Introducing the Selection

1. Ask children if, on a summer night, they have ever seen a firefly (sometimes called lightning bug, or lightning beetle) darting around and blinking on and off, here and there. If they have, let several tell about it. Perhaps some of them have even caught a bug in their cupped hands to peek at when it lights up in the dark space between their palms.
2. If no one raises the question, ask pupils how they think the bugs can make their lights. (The light is made by a chemical *luciferin* when it is combined with oxygen in the presence of another chemical. The production of this cold light is a complex process that occurs in the body of the firefly. *The World Book Encyclopedia* gives an understandable description of the process.)
3. Try to have a fairly large photograph of a firefly to show to those

children who have not seen one. (*Our Wonderful World Encyclopedia* has a suitable one.)

4. Ask the children to open their books to page 15 and to look at the picture. Have them point out the fireflies and discuss what they are doing. Then tell the children to listen, as you read the poem, in order to find out how the poet describes a firefly. Read the entire poem twice without interruption. After the first reading, just tell the children you will read it again. (Most poems need at least two readings: once to get the general overall idea and then once to grasp the idea from the beginning and to note interesting aspects.)

POST-READING EXTENSION

Exploring the Selection

Questions to ask
1. Ask children how the firefly is described in the poem ("... a little bug all lit/And made to go on wings.") Ask them if they could have "thought of it." (Some may say, "Yes"!)
2. Then ask the pupils to tell who is talking in the poem. (The poet is writing of her own childhood; therefore, it is a little girl. Many of the poems for children are written in the first person, and children can identify themselves with the "I.")
3. Ask pupils to tell about other flying bugs they know, like bees and flies and mosquitoes. Compare their qualities with the firefly, and help the children appreciate the beauty of the firefly.
4. Let pupils stretch their imaginations by asking them what the "little light" might see up in the sky.

Interpreting Literature

Simplicity and repetition
1. This poem is elegantly simple in its wording, so that the effect is one of poetic beauty. Note also the graceful repetition in the first stanza, and call it to the attention of the children. Ask them to listen as you read just the first two lines, and to note especially the repetition of "is going." Then read the first three lines, asking children to note the repetition of "a little light."

Mood
2. Ask pupils how they think the little girl feels when she sees the firefly. (Answers will vary, but try to stimulate the idea of awe, wonder, or puzzlement.) See if pupils can tell the part of the poem that gives them this idea. ("I never could have thought of it.") Note the number of long sounds for vowels (*light, going, by, see, sky*) in the first stanza. They give the stanza a slow, dreamy quality. The short vowel sounds in the second stanza (*never, thought, it, bug, lit*) quicken the pace and give the stanza a crisp, rather final treatment with the line, "To have a little bug all lit." The last line of the poem slows only slightly, leaving the idea suspended just

a bit at the end. (Therefore, when you read the poem, do not drop your voice too much on the last *wings*; instead, give the word emphasis.)

Developing Language Skills

Vocabulary development 1. The words in this poem should not be difficult for children once firefly has been explained. However, the poem ought to stimulate children to wonder about other insects and bugs they know. You might start by suggesting, "I wonder why—the butterfly alights on flowers, or why bees hum, or why mosquitoes sting." The discussion should give children a chance to express their ideas and to gain additional concepts. If you have pictures of flying insects and bugs, show them for additional discussion.

Interpretive activities 2. Now bring the discussion back to the firefly and see if any child can say the poem alone. Let volunteers try, and then have the whole class say the poem together. No formal attempt should be made to have poems memorized, but after repeated reading and discussion, many children can say the poems, at least with a little help.

Children might enjoy illustrating this poem, and you might put out some dark blue paper and colored chalk as well as tempera paints and crayons. The pictures would make an attractive bulletin-board display, with the poem written on tagboard and the illustrations mounted around it. Later you can have children choose the picture they want to put on the tagboard with the poem.

Research activities 3. Ask children to be on the lookout for pictures or information about fireflies to report to the class.

Books to read 4. Have a copy of Elizabeth Madox Roberts' *Under the Tree* available for children to use in browsing and for you to use in reading aloud to them. Try to get some picture books about insects, such as *We Like Bugs* by Gladys Conklin, or *Everyday Insects* by Gertrude Allen.

also — *favorite place*

Lucky Ladybugs

One Is Good but Two Are Better

PAGES 16–27

PRE-READING PREPARATION

Background for the Selection

This selection has been abridged from the original book *One Is Good but Two Are Better* by Louis Slobodkin. The selection omits one episode and some explanatory sections in order to have a workable selection for the children. The story poem is realistic in its theme of friendship and the mutual need of human beings. The activities mentioned, like pulling wagons, swinging, playing ball, or hide-and-seek, are common experiences for many children.

The author-artist Louis Slobodkin won the Caldecott Award for his illustrations of James Thurber's *Many Moons*. He has also illustrated *The Hundred Dresses* and the popular Moffat books, all by Eleanor Estes. His illustrations are pastel washes with soft outlines but with plenty of action. They allow the child to use his imagination.

Elements of Literature

This writer uses a style common to several of the picture books for children—that of rhymed verse. The selection is really narrative poetry, and it must meet the same requirements as other poetry, though its main purpose is to tell a story.

These poetical requirements include rhythm, cadence, movement, sound, melody, imagery, and figurative language. In this selection, the following literary (poetical) qualities are exemplified:

1. the regularity of the rhythm that propels the reader forward.
2. the short vowel sounds and rhymes that create a matter-of-fact tone.
3. the imagery evoked by the every-day activities.

Introducing the Selection

1. Ask the class what they do when they go home after school. Then ask them if they play by themselves or if they have brothers or sisters or friends to play with them. Get the children to tell what they do when they play alone and when they play with others. If children play in the streets, as many city children do, get them to see the difference between being an onlooker in a group as

others play and actually doing the playing themselves. This story tells about the actual playing.

2. Note that this is a story-poem and that it rhymes. Ask children to listen for words that sound alike as the story is read aloud.

3. Ask children for the meaning of words that may be unfamiliar to them, like *rough*, *oar*, *row*, *lag*, and *peek*. Since the context and illustrations give hints, you may wish to delay this explanation until *after* the first reading. The following definitions may be helpful:

rough: not smooth; not level; not even
oar: a long pole with a flat end, used in rowing
row: use oars to move a boat
lag: move too slowly; fall behind
peek: look quickly and slyly; peep

4. Have the children open their books to page 16. They will follow the pictures as you read each page. Direct them to turn the pages when you do, so that they will be on the right page. For the first reading, go right through the whole story, without stopping to talk about the different parts or pictures.

POST-READING EXTENSION

Exploring the Selection

Sharing Time   Direct pupils to turn to page 27, where the Sharing Time activities are listed. Read each question and identify it by number. Let the children turn back to the story to formulate their answers.
The following are answers to the Sharing Time questions:

1. Children might first name the activities at random. Then review the sequence of the activities in the story (letter, wagon, swing, boat, ball, tag, hide-and-seek, sing, play). For their drawing, some children may draw only one activity, or they may draw several on one page. If a child draws each activity on a separate page, these could be stapled together to make a booklet to take home and/or to use in retelling the story.

2. Accept any of the combinations: *better-letter, enough-rough, sun-fun, shore-oar, friends-ends, bat-that, lag-tag, peek-seek, more-four, play-day*. Or, if it is necessary, give one word as the stimulus for the children to give the rhyming word. Use all the possibilities in the story.

3. This question should elicit the theme of the story, even though some children might think they are to retell the story. Any answer including cooperation between two individuals would be acceptable. Try to get a general statement rather than something like "It takes two to play ball."

Following are additional questions to supplement those already asked:

1. What makes you think the two children who play together are friends? (The idea that some of the activities must be done in unison, or at least on the spot, would indicate at least some level of friendship and cooperation.)
2. What other games or activities can you think of that take two people? (Children might suggest playing train or store or house, teeter-tottering, or some of the games that are in the classroom.)
3. What do you play at home with baby brothers and sisters? with older brothers and sisters? (This will extend the child's thinking beyond the story situation to his own, and he may suggest rocking the baby's cradle, talking to him, shaking his rattle, and so on. With older children, he may be the pupil when playing school, or the patient when playing hospital.)

Interpreting Literature

Rhythm 1. The rhythm of this story-poem is very definite, with a beat that does not change throughout the whole selection. The lines are short, which creates a forward motion, and the use of one-syllable words gives a clipped finish to each episode. Ask the children to tap the beat as you read a few verses, two beats to the line (with the exception of page 21, where "You can row / 'round the world" must be treated as one line). If you wish, you can contrast the staccato beat with a swinging one, and then ask the children which beat reminds them of running and playing.

Sounds and rhyme 2. The rhyming words, with the exception of *better* and *letter*, are all one-syllable words. The shortness of the words creates a feeling of definiteness, of motion, and of completeness. Ask the children to repeat the rhymes and listen not only to the sound but to the way it makes them feel. (You may need to suggest fast or slow, lazy or busy.) Then ask them if it sounds real or make-believe. Since children ought to recognize the reality of the situations (even the make-believe rowing around the world is a play activity in real life), they can begin to sense the way tone affects idea.

Imagery 3. Imagery in this poem is created by the illustrations and by the simple activities that are in the experience of most children of this age. In case they are not, then you must build the imagery through pictures, discussion, and demonstration. One way would be to have pairs of children pantomime each activity, with the class guessing which activity it is. Different ways to pantomime the same idea can also be tried.

Developing Language Skills

Vocabulary development 1. Much of what has been done thus far is really oral-language development. Vocabulary can be extended by discussing the words listed in item three of the "Introducing the Selection" section, if you did not do so at that time. You might also give other words to rhyme with the story rhymes (*better, letter, setter; enough, rough, tough;* etc.). Words selected might be nonsense words, but if a real word is given, discuss its meaning with the children.

Interpretive activities 2. In addition to pantomiming, children could dramatize the episodes in the story, making up appropriate conversation to suit the purpose.

Ask children to draw activities they might carry out with a friend. The picture could be used as the basis for telling the group what the pupil had in mind.

Research activities 3. Have children collect games that two or more can play, and start a chart of these to keep in the room.

Books to read 4. Have copies of *One Is Good but Two Are Better* by Louis Slobodkin on the reading table and call attention to those parts of the book omitted here in the text. Let children compare their ideas with the author's. You could also put out *Two Is a Team* by Jerrold and Lorraine Beim; *The Snowy Day* and *Peter's Chair* by Ezra Jack Keats; *A Wish for Little Sister* by Jacqueline Ayer; *Play with Me* by Marie Hall Ets; or *Nobody Plays with a Cabbage* by Meindert DeJong.

Audio-visual aids 5. The following audio-visual aids are recommended for use with this selection:

Let's Share a Seesaw, in the *Schools and Sharing* series.   10-minute color film. McGraw-Hill Films. Shows an integrated group of children with older children helping younger ones.

Finders Keepers.   Color and sound filmstrip. Weston Woods Studios. Tells how two quarreling puppies learn to share a bone. By Will and Nicolas.

Robert's Family and Their Neighbors, in the series entitled *Robert and His Family.*   8-minute color and sound filmstrip. Society for Visual Education, Inc. Shows how Robert, a little Negro boy, lives and shares with his family and neighbors.

Tommy

PRE-READING PREPARATION

Background for the Selection

This poem is taken from the book of poems entitled *Bronzeville Boys and Girls* by Gwendolyn Brooks. Each poem is about a child, and this one is about Tommy. Gwendolyn Brooks is a well-known Negro poet who has received several awards and prizes for her works, including the Pulitzer Prize and two Guggenheim Fellowships.

"Tommy" is a simple, short poem about a boy who plants a seed and cares for it, only to have it come up without his knowing it. The experience is a familiar one to many children, and the poem reports the experience plainly and directly until the last two lines, when there is a shift from the child to the seed. The delight of the poem comes with this surprise ending.

Elements of Literature

This poem records the experience of one child planting a seed; it does so with a minimum of imagery, but with a recounting of action in a regular rhythm and an *a b c b* rhyme scheme (that is, only the second and fourth lines rhyme). The following literary aspects of this poem are selected for discussion with the children:
   1. the pattern formed by the rhythm and rhyme.
   2. the surprise ending.

Introducing the Selection

1. Tell the children that the title of the poem you are going to read is "Tommy." Let them guess what the poem might be about. You can give them a hint that it is something Tommy does.
2. If no one guesses that Tommy is planting something, ask children to tell what they did last summer and see if they mention gardening. If no one does (and city children may have had no experience with this), have children open their books to pages 28–29 and look at the pictures.
3. Call attention to the picture of Tommy's activities, and let children discuss comparable experiences.

4. Tell pupils there is a surprise in the poem and see if they can find it as you read the poem to them.

POST-READING EXTENSION

Exploring the Selection

Questions to ask 1. Ask children what the surprise is. (Some may say, "The seed popped out," but this is not so good an answer as, "The seed came up without *consulting* Tommy." Children may say this word without knowing what it means.)
2. What does the poem mean when it says, "My seed had popped itself right out, / Without consulting me"? "Who is *me*?" (Children should realize Tommy is talking, and they may be able to guess the meaning of *consulting.* If they cannot, ask leading questions such as, "Does your mother *consult* you when you go to a drive-in or drugstore or ice-cream store to see what you want to eat?" "Are you *consulted* regarding which TV program you wish to see?" The dictionary definition for this use of the word is:

consulting: taking into consideration; having regard for

Help children put this meaning into the poem so that they get the idea of Tommy's thinking his seed should not have come up without first asking him.
3. Ask children to tell what seeds need in order to make them grow. (Heat, soil, and water, so that plants can get started and later make their own food.) Then check the poem to see if Tommy took care of his seed properly. (He "watered it and cared for it.")
4. How do you think Tommy felt when he saw his seed had come up? (Children may say he was surprised to see it so soon, angry because the seed had not asked him, and happy that it grew.)
5. Let children suggest what they think happened next. (Perhaps Tommy cared for the plant until it grew big.)

Interpreting Literature

Pattern 1. The rhythm in this poem does not skip a beat from beginning to end. Ask the children to tap as you read the poem again, tapping first on the second word, *put,* then continuing with every other syllable. There are four beats in lines one and three and three beats in lines two and four. You might draw lines on the blackboard as the children tap (/ / / / for the first line, / / / for the second, and so on).
Then ask the children which words rhyme (*grow—know* and *see—me*). Notice that the rhyming words are at the end of the second and fourth lines. Let children give other words that rhyme with these, or let them give other rhyming pairs.

<table>
<tr><td>Surprise ending</td><td>2.</td><td>The surprise at the end of the poem results from the use of the word *popped*, instead of *came*, and from the idea expressed by *consulting*. Ask the children why the poet said the seed "popped" and let them describe the way they think the seed came up. (They might demonstrate by squatting down and "popping" themselves up.) Discuss why a seed should "consult" the one who planted it. Try to help children attain some awareness of the pressure of growth that is natural when the prerequisites are present. (The seed can no more control its growth than the children can control theirs. This understanding is background for the humor in the *consulting* concept.)</td></tr>
</table>

Developing Language Skills

<table>
<tr><td>Vocabulary development</td><td>1.</td><td>Children have already discussed *popped* and *consulting*. You might extend their vocabularies by asking them what vegetable or flower Tommy's plant might be. This would give them a chance to learn the names of other plants. If you have a seed catalog, pupils can identify the pictures. Children at this age sometimes do not have the names (labels) for fruits and vegetables they have eaten.</td></tr>
<tr><td>Interpretive activities</td><td>2.</td><td>Read the poem again and ask children to say it with you whenever they can. This poem is harder to remember than some others they have had. The poem lends itself to illustration, and children could draw one picture for a part of the poem or a series of four pictures for the total poem (one each for planting, watering, caring for the plant by perhaps pulling weeds, and then seeing it pop out).</td></tr>
<tr><td>Research activities</td><td>3.</td><td>The class might plant a seed in a flowerpot and watch it grow. Corn and bean seeds usually sprout quite easily. Pupils might be able to see the plant pop out.</td></tr>
<tr><td>Books to read</td><td>4.</td><td>Have available a copy of *Bronzeville Boys and Girls* by Gwendolyn Brooks, and read the poems describing some of the other boys and girls. You might also get *Nobody Plays with a Cabbage* by Meindert DeJong, and *Bits That Grow Big* and *Travelers All*, both by Irma E. Webber.</td></tr>
<tr><td>Audio-visual aids</td><td>5.</td><td>The following audio-visual aid is recommended for use with this selection:
Finding Out How Plants Grow, in the *Basic Primary Science* series. Color filmstrip. Society for Visual Education, Inc. Shows how a bean plant grows.</td></tr>
</table>

The Little Red Hen and the Grain of Wheat

PAGES 30–45

PRE-READING PREPARATION

Background for the Selection

This well-known folktale is presented in the version retold by Veronica S. Hutchinson from her collection entitled *Chimney Corner Stories*. She has preserved the terseness of the tale in her version, and she has restated the action at the end of each episode after the Little Red Hen has said, "I will." Some other versions do not restate the action; instead they merely state, "And she did."

Folktales have been handed down orally for generations until some individual recorded them in writing or on records or tape. Folktales arose from a simple society. They deal with everyday happenings. Because they were first told rather than read, the tales in their evolution have been stripped of any superfluous description, and the action has become paramount. Otherwise, the storyteller would have lost his audience. This folktale of the Little Red Hen is a good example, showing the economy of detail. The sequence from planting the seed to eating the bread was typical of the process a generation ago, though today the cutting and threshing may be done in one operation with a combine.

a couple of generations ago ?

Elements of Literature

The story pattern of the folktale follows a typical sequence: a short introduction that gives time, place, characters, and problem; the development of the problem in a series of incidents that are sometimes repetitive, sometimes accumulative; and a quick, definite solution as the climax. After the climax, a sentence or two (called *anti-climax*) is often provided to taper off the story. "The Little Red Hen" has several folktale characteristics that will be considered here:

1. the story pattern as typical.
2. the repetition of the action.
3. the implied moral.

Introducing the Selection

1. Show a picture of a red hen if you can find one. Ask children what they know about hens in general. They may say hens live on a

farm, lay eggs, and have baby chicks. Ask pupils if they know what hens eat. If the children do not know, tell them that hens eat wheat, corn, and other grains. Chickens also eat bread and crumbs, just as some birds do. Hens are also industrious in their scratching about for bits to eat, and they appear to be busy all day long.

2. Ask if anyone knows what it means to "thresh wheat." Some children may be familiar with this process of separating the wheat from its outer coat and stem. Discussion about threshing can be continued after the story has been read.

3. Tell the children that this is an old, old story that has been told to children for many years, to their grandparents when they were little boys and girls, and even before that.

4. Have children open their books to page 30 and let them look at all the pictures for the story. Then ask them to turn back to the beginning, and tell them that they can follow the pictures as you read the story aloud. Children are likely to chime in on the repetitive parts unless you suggest that the first time around they are to listen to you read. Tell them you will read it again, and they all can help then. If there is a reader in the group, this is a good story on which to let him show his prowess, though he should not be expected to read words like *scratching, grain, thresh, ground, flour,* and *shared* without prior help. Read the story a second time so the children can act as chorus for the repetitive parts.

POST-READING EXTENSION

Exploring the Selection

Sharing Time Turn to the Sharing Time page and have pupils react to the ideas.

1. Pupils should understand the steps in the process (planting, cutting, threshing, and grinding the wheat, making and baking the bread). You may write each one on the chalkboard as the children tell you. In case they do not get the sequence, reread the needed portion of the story. Have the children draw a series of pictures on paper to show what the Little Red Hen did, or have different children make a picture for only one of the steps. These can be mounted on the bulletin board or made into one picture booklet.

2. Children will see the justice of reward for effort; they will probably say that the other animals did not help, so they should not have the treat.

3. The fact that the Little Red Hen shared the bread with her chicks is stated; the children should recognize this as an indication of being a good mother. They might also say that the hen was a good

mother because she worked to make the bread for the chicks and prevented the others from eating the bread.

Additional questions if time permits You might also ask the following questions:

1. What did you learn about the other animals in the story? (They were lazy and uncooperative.)
2. How do you think the duck, cat, and dog felt when the hen and her chicks ate the bread? (Perhaps they were envious and wished they had some bread; perhaps they were sorry that they had not helped; perhaps they were glad for the Little Red Hen, because she deserved the bread for her work.)
3. What do you think the duck, cat, and dog did the next time the Little Red Hen asked for help? (Some may think the animals have reformed; others may be skeptical. Get children to justify their answers and tell why they answered as they did.)
4. Can you think of a time when you acted like the duck and cat and dog? What happened? (They may suggest not having helped in connection with a picnic, barbecue, clean-up, or baby-sitting; yet they wanted the treat without working for it.)

Interpreting Literature

Story pattern
1. The folktale pattern is followed in this story. Ask the children to note the beginning, which tells the time (one day), the place (farmyard), the character (Little Red Hen), and the problem (to plant the wheat). Then ask the children to tell how many times the hen asked the others to help (actually six, counting the last). If necessary, refer back to the story and the pictures in order to find the answers. Then ask children where the high point of the story, or the real surprise (climax), comes (with the hen's answer of "Oh no, you won't!"). Note that in the end (the anti-climax) the hen is sharing the bread with her chicks, leaving all the readers and listeners satisfied.

Repetition
2. The repetition of the question-answer pattern (with only the slight changes that keep the action moving) makes the story easy to remember and easy to retell. The most difficult part is the sequence of the process, which may be unfamiliar to children. The pictures in the book will help children follow the sequence. If the repetitive parts were discussed under the previous item, it is not necessary to repeat them here.

Moral
3. The ethic of folktales is clear-cut and simple. Right must triumph, and the villain must be punished. In this story, the positive virtues of industry and consideration (the hen did ask the others if they wanted to do the job) were rewarded, though not stated explicitly. Ask the children what they think the lesson of the story is and see if they can tell why they think so. While the main purpose of the story is enjoyment, children do absorb the ethical values inherent in the stories; but sometimes the less that is actually said, the better the lesson is learned.

Developing Language Skills

Vocabulary development   1. Continue the discussion about threshing if the class seems to need additional information. Pictures of the modern combines would be helpful, although the old-fashioned methods should also be described. It would be a practical learning experience if children could see wheat with the stalks and chaff on, and then see how beating the heads removes the outer coat. Another concept that may need to be developed is the grinding of the wheat into flour. A mortar and pestle and a few grains could be used to demonstrate the idea, although pictures would also be useful. The discussion might also start with the miller, who mills, continue with the baker, who bakes, and then deal with other occupations that indicate what people do (farmer, storekeeper, teacher, and others).

Interpretive activities   2. Have children act out the story, letting each child have a turn to be in the play. (Some children may be chicks, too.) Let them pantomime the actions and say the words that are actually in the story.

Research activities   3. Children may want to collect pictures of the animals mentioned. Different parts of the bulletin board could be used for pictures of hens, chicks, ducks, cats, and dogs. The various breeds of dogs, for example, might be mentioned, also, in order to extend the children's vocabularies and experiences. If you wish, the idea could be extended to various farm animals.

Books to read   4. Have available a copy of Veronica Hutchinson's *Chimney Corner Stories,* since this is the source of the story. Other stories about hens and ducks include *The Cock, the Mouse, and the Little Red Hen* by Félicité Lefèvre; *The Speckled Hen: A Russian Nursery Rhyme* by Harve Zemach; *Make Way for Ducklings* by Robert McCloskey; and *The Story About Ping* and *Angus and the Ducks* by Marjorie Flack.

Audio-visual aids   5. The following audio-visual aids are recommended for use with this selection:
The Little Red Hen. 11-minute film. Coronet Films. Contains pictures and live activities of the characters.
The Little Red Hen and the Grain of Wheat, in the *Children's Classics* series. 11-minute color and sound filmstrip. Society for Visual Education, Inc. Includes sound effects of the barnyard.

Jack and Jill

PAGE 46

PRE-READING PREPARATION

Background for the Selection

This rhyme, which is one of the most familiar of all the Mother Goose rhymes, has an interesting history. According to *The Annotated Mother Goose*, by William S. and Ceil Baring-Gould, the woodcuts that illustrated "Jack and Gill" (as it was then spelled) in the original *Mother Goose's Melody* showed two boys instead of a boy and a girl. As many as fourteen stanzas were later added to the rhyme, but the first one is still the most popular. Although Mother Goose rhymes have been associated with political figures and events in English history, the appeal of the rhymes to modern children is based upon the qualities inherent in the rhymes themselves.

Elements of Literature

Mother Goose rhymes contain the same literary elements found in poetry, although the rhymes vary in literary quality just as poetry does. The aspects to be considered in this rhyme are:
1. the rhythm and cadence in relation to the action.
2. the similar sounds, including rhyming words and alliteration.

Introducing the Selection

1. Ask the children if they know any Mother Goose rhymes and let them say some of the ones they know. If anyone says "Jack and Jill," just accept it and continue on.
2. Ask the pupils who Mother Goose is. They may have several different answers, depending on the books they have seen. If you have several Mother Goose books available, show the various pictures of the lady as depicted by the illustrators. (A familiar concept is an old lady riding through the air on a goose.) Tell the children that some people think Mother Goose was an English nursemaid who said rhymes to the children in her care.
3. Tell the children that Mother Goose rhymes are very old and sometimes contain words we do not often use today. However, they can try to guess the meanings of the words from the ideas given in the rhymes.

4. Direct the children to open their books to page 46 and look at the picture. If someone has already said "Jack and Jill," let the children acknowledge this. Then say that the rhymes are not always printed the same way in all the books. Ask them to listen as you read the rhyme to see if it is like the one they know. (In some versions, *get* is used in place of *fetch*.)

POST-READING EXTENSION

Exploring the Selection

Questions to ask

1. Check with children to see if the version in the text is the same as the one they know. Note any differences.
2. Ask someone to tell in his own words what Jack and Jill did. (They went up the hill to get some water, and on the way down, Jack fell and hurt his head. Jill also fell down.) You may wish to check the meaning of *fetch* and *crown* at this time. (See the "Developing Language Skills" section later in this lesson.)
3. Let children guess what happened when Jack and Jill got home. (They may suggest that Jack got first-aid treatment; that Jack and Jill were scolded for being careless; and so on.)
4. Ask children if they have ever had to go after water. (Perhaps they have been on a farm or in a park, on a camping trip or picnic where they needed to get water in a pail or bucket.) Let them describe their experiences, including how heavy it is to carry a pail of water. (If anyone is skeptical, you might fill a plastic bucket— the gallon ice-cream type—and let him see.)
5. Then ask pupils why they think Jack fell down and pulled Jill with him. (Going downhill with a bucket full of water is not so easy, even when two are carrying it. So if Jack fell and Jill was also holding onto the bucket, she would get pulled down, too.)

Interpreting Literature

Rhythm

1. The rhythm of the poem is clipped and definite, due in part to the many one-syllable words. Ask two or three children to "step off" the rhyme, using one step for each word, except *water* and *after*. (Each of these needs two steps.) Other children can slap their knees in time. The very regular beat of this poem makes it easy to say. Note how the cadence seems to ascend with the first two lines and descend on the last two. Ask children if they can tell why this is done. (To show going up and down the hill.)

Sounds and rhyme

2. The rhyming words *Jill—hill* and *down—crown* can be noted as you start to say the poem. Have children fill in the needed word. You might say, "Jack and Jill/Went up the _____," or even omit *Jill* if the rhyme is well known. Do the same with *down* and *crown*. Then note the alliteration (the repetition of the same sound at the

beginning of words) of *Jack* and *Jill*. Ask children for other words that begin the same way. The distinction between words that start alike and that end alike, or rhyme, is not clear to some children at this age; therefore, practice is good.

Developing Language Skills

Vocabulary development 1. The two words probably not familiar to children are:

fetch: go and get; bring
crown: head

Since *fetch* is used in some parts of the country today, it may not be a new word for some children. Regional differences are also apparent in the use of *pail* and *bucket*. Children may mention other differences in words they know, such as *square* and *block*.

Interpretive activities 2. Let all children say the rhyme in unison until they can stay together quite well. Then choose two children to pantomime the action as the rest of the class says the poem. Several pairs of children can try, and appropriate actions can be praised.

You might wish to introduce stanzas two and three of the rhyme, for these are not in many of the Mother Goose books:

Up Jack got, and home did trot,
    As fast as he could caper,
To old Dame Dob, who patched his nob,
    With vinegar and brown paper.

When Gill came in, how she did grin,
    To see Jack's paper plaster;
Dame Dob, vexed, did whip her next
    For causing Jack's disaster.

(From *The Annotated Mother Goose,* pp. 58–59.)

Research activities 3. Ask children to find pictures of Mother Goose in various Mother Goose books, then plan time to compare these. Have children also find "Jack and Jill" in the various books and see how the pictures are alike or different. (You might use different colored slips of paper to mark the pages, one color for Mother Goose and one for Jack and Jill.)

Books to read 4. Some of the titles and illustrators of Mother Goose Books currently in print are: *Real Mother Goose,* Blanche Fisher Wright; *Mother Goose,* Tasha Tudor; *Ring O'Roses,* Leslie Brooke; *In a Pumpkin Shell,* Joan Walsh Anglund; *Brian Wildsmith's Mother Goose;* Caldecott picture books; and *Book of Nursery and Mother Goose Rhymes* and *A Pocketful of Posies,* both by Marguerite de Angeli.

L. Leslie?

Audio-visual aids 5. The following audio-visual aids are recommended for use:
Jack and Jill.   Color filmstrip. Eye Gate House, Inc.
Jack and Jill.   Color-sound filmstrip. Jam Handy School Service.

Humpty Dumpty

PAGE 47

PRE-READING PREPARATION

Background for the Selection

This Mother Goose rhyme is really a riddle, and the answer is "an egg." Like other Mother Goose rhymes, "Humpty Dumpty" has several versions, but the one in the text is the best known today. In a version published in 1803, the last line read, "Could not set Humpty Dumpty up again." Some scholars believe that the age of this rhyme is "to be measured in thousands of years." From time to time, the name has been associated with political figures, and the name is often given to a short, clumsy person. It is also the name of a girls' game, according to the Baring-Goulds, authors of *The Annotated Mother Goose*. There are translated versions of the rhyme in France, Sweden, Denmark, Finland, Switzerland, and Germany.

Elements of Literature

The appeal of this verse (and it is a popular one with children) is primarily in the sounds of the words and in the rhythm. The riddle is secondary, even though it is expressed in a unique way. The following literary elements will be given attention in this lesson:
1. the sounds and repetition of sounds.
2. the rhythm and cadence.
3. the imagery evoked, especially in the last line.

Introducing the Selection

1. Tell the children that this poem is another Mother Goose rhyme. You might review what they already know about Mother Goose, and have them recite "Jack and Jill."
2. Tell the pupils that this rhyme is really a riddle—meaning a puzzling question or problem—and that maybe they can guess what the answer is after you have read it. Some who know the verse may not know that it is a riddle.
3. Ask the children to open their books to page 47 and look at the picture. They might point out various details in the picture. Then tell them to listen, as you read, to see if they can figure out who Humpty Dumpty really is.

POST-READING EXTENSION

Exploring the Selection

Questions to ask 1. See if anyone can guess who Humpty Dumpty is. Though the picture shows him sitting on the wall before his fall, he is not particularly recognizable as an egg.
2. Ask why it would be hard to put Humpty Dumpty back together again. (The shell is all broken and the bits could not easily be put together.)
3. Discuss the reason for saying "All the King's horses and all the King's men." (Humpty Dumpty was so "broken" that even this large group couldn't put him back together again. Earlier versions say, "threescore men and threescore more"—120 men—couldn't do it; and if these groups cannot, the implication is that no one can.)
4. Ask the children if they have ever broken anything (besides an egg) that couldn't be put back together again. Let them tell about it. (They might mention toys that cannot be glued, balloons, bottles, and so on.)

Interpreting Literature

Sounds 1. The *ump* sound in *Humpty Dumpty* is fun to say because it is explosive and tickles the lips as a humming sound is made. Let the children say "Humpty Dumpty" over and over several times in order to feel this. The *pty* takes good lip and tongue action; as pupils are saying this, check to see they are not saying "Humpy Dumpy." Ask the children for rhyming words ("words that sound alike at the end") and elicit three pairs from the rhyme: *Humpty—Dumpty*, *wall—fall*, and *men—again*. Ask which words are repeated. (*Humpty Dumpty* and *all the King's.*)

Rhythm and cadence 2. Note the difference in the pace of the first part of the verse in comparison to the last part. (The first is quick and regular; the last part, especially the last line, is slower and more clumsy to say than the first part.) Ask children which part they think is easier to say and see if they can tell why. (It takes tongue action to say "all the King's horses.")

Imagery 3. The first part of the verse is pictured in the text. Ask the children how they would illustrate the last part. (Lots of men on horses looking at a broken egg.) The answers will tell you whether or not the phrase "all the King's horses" was meaningful to the children. If there seems to be confusion, explain that the King used an army of men on horseback to defend his castle. (Some suitable pictures of knights in armor would help clarify this idea.)

Developing Language Skills

Vocabulary development 1. Since words recall different mental images, let children tell about other kinds of *walls* than that pictured. (They may mention walls

53

of the schoolroom, cement walls, stone walls, and walls around a castle or town, depending on their experiences.)

Interpretive activities 2. Let half the class be Humpty Dumpty and pretend to fall off their chairs while the other half says the verse. Then reverse the groups so everyone has a chance. Children like dramatic play, and such a simple activity they find humorous. Each child might also make an illustration for the rhyme, though the last part of the rhyme would be difficult for most of them to draw.

Research activities 3. Have pupils look in several Mother Goose books to find out how Humpty Dumpty is pictured. Ask them to choose the one they like best. A discussion about their choices would serve as a fine oral language lesson. Pupils might also be on the lookout for pictures of walls and mounted men.

Books to read 4. In addition to the Mother Goose books listed for the "Jack and Jill" rhyme, try to get a copy of Kate Greenaway's *Mother Goose*, for the Humpty Dumpty pictured there is a little boy.

The Little Elfman

PAGE 48

PRE-READING PREPARATION

Background for the Selection

Fanciful creatures hold charm for young children, and elves are among the most interesting, for they are tiny beings, often full of mischief. They are sometimes pictured as lithe and agile, with pointed caps, pointed-toed shoes, and jesters' costumes. Their eyes are merry, and they seem to be coiled like springs, ready to move about or jump at a moment's notice. In different countries, different attributes have been associated with them. Some elves have good qualities and others not, but even those who are good and helpful may be a bit saucy or peevish. This poem, written by John Kendrick Bangs, is one of the favorites.

Elements of Literature

The turn of a phrase, often at the end of a poem, serves to complete the thought; in addition, it leaves the reader thinking about the idea and its cleverness or accuracy. This seeing of an ordinary phenomenon from an unusual point of view is one of the characteristics that lift poetry to an imaginative, higher plane than would a usual, prosaic approach. The last two lines of "The Little Elfman" are an example of this, and children should be helped to recognize the contribution these lines make to the total poem. The emphasis, therefore, in a discussion of this poem focuses on:

1. the unusual turn of an idea that creates a surprise ending.
2. the rhyme scheme.
3. the rhythm and accent.

Introducing the Selection

1. Ask the children what is usually the first thing said to them by an older person who has not seen them for a while. Try to get from children the idea of how they have grown. You might discuss relative sizes at different ages and the difference in size among people the same age, for these are topics of interest to young children.
2. Then turn to fairy folk of little size and ask pupils what they know

about elves. Someone may be familiar with "The Shoemaker and the Elves" story, but try to get children to visualize how small an elf might be. There seems to be no agreement as to the exact size of elves, though the *Encyclopedia Americana* states that they are about the size of a young girl's thumb. However, their size belies their strength and ability to perform difficult tasks.

3. Ask children to open their books to page 48 and look at the picture of the elf. Let them comment on his size in relation to other objects pictured there.

4. Tell pupils to listen, as you read the poem, in order to find out what the elfman has to say about his size.

POST-READING EXTENSION

Exploring the Selection

Questions to ask 1. After you have read the poem once or maybe twice, ask: What did the elfman say about his size? (He is just as big for him as you are big for you.) To whom was he talking? (The author of the poem, but also any reader who identifies himself with the "I" in the poem.)

2. What is the elfman trying to tell you in the last two lines of the poem? (That each is a size that is right for him.)

3. Why do you think the elfman frowned when he answered? (He was a bit annoyed or bothered by the question, because anyone ought to know he was the right size.)

4. What makes you think the elfman might be mischievous or proud? (The sauciness of his quick retort, though children will probably say, "The way he answered.")

5. What do you say when people tell you, "My, how you've grown!"? (Answers will vary. Some children may like the attention they thus get, while others wish adults would not say this. What else does one expect of children this age, but to grow?)

6. If you wish, you might ask if there are other ways than size of showing how "big" one is. (This concept of maturity should include, at the five- and six-year-old level, such behavior as taking turns, not pushing and shoving, waiting to speak, sharing materials, and so on, but try not to be too moralistic about it all.)

Interpreting Literature

Surprise ending 1. The last two lines of the poem contain the surprise ending that lifts the poem above the ordinary. Ask children what in the poem gives them a new idea. To help them see from an elfman's point of view, have children look at different levels and report what they see—from sitting-on-the-floor level, from sitting-on-a-chair level, from a standing level, from at-the-top-of-the-steps level, and so on.

Rhyme	2. Notice the "said he" instead of "he said" that makes an internal (within the line) rhyme with *me*. Ask children to listen for the rhyming words: *blow—grow, through—you*. (This *a b c b* pattern of the rhyme scheme is a popular pattern in rhymes for children.)
Rhythm and accent	3. Notice the regularity of the accent that carries the movement along. The poem scans exactly; however, the cadence is not choppy, but, instead, smooth. Therefore, you will want to prevent a sing-song way of saying it. You might let children move their hands up and down to the rhythm (two down beats per line) in order for them to get the idea. Though this is an exaggerated approach, it should dramatize both the rhythm and accent (beat) of the poem. Then reread the poem without the motions.

Developing Language Skills

Vocabulary development	1. In addition to *elf* and *elfman*, another word needing definition in this poem is:

pictures not fit this

lilies: plants that grow from bulbs. Their flowers are usually large, bell-shaped, and beautiful. Often, the flowers are divided into six parts. *(like tiger lilies)* *field* *calla lilies are shown*

If possible, have pictures of several types of lilies for children to see. (Seed catalogues, the dictionary, and the encyclopedia are good sources.) Compare the size of the flowers with the elfman.

Interpretive activities	2. Since you have said this poem several times already, ask children to say it with you this time. Then let one group be "I" and say the first verse, and another group be "he" and say the second verse. You may also ask one child to be the elfman, and have the other children say the rest of the poem.
	Let pupils draw a picture, either to illustrate the poem or to put the elfman in some other setting. You could put the poem in manuscript writing on tagboard and mount the pictures and the poem on the bulletin board. Later, one illustration could be chosen to paste on the tagboard, and the tagboard could become a page in a Big Book (looseleaf) that you and the class are making.
Research activities	3. Ask children to be on the lookout for pictures and stories about elves. Maybe parents will help them find out about elves.
Books to read	4. This poem is included in several collections, such as *Childcraft*, and *All the Silver Pennies* by Blanche Jennings Thompson, both with illustrations. Pictures of elves are also found in *The Shoemaker and the Elves*, illustrated by Adrienne Adams, or in *Grimm's Popular Stories*, where the same story is illustrated by George Cruikshank. You might also get *No Fighting, No Biting!* by Else Minarik and *The Smallest Boy in the Class* by Jerrold Beim.
Audio-visual aids	5. The following audio-visual aid is recommended for use: *The Land of Make-Believe*, in the set *The Child's World of Poetry— Group 1.* Record and color study print. Society for Visual Education, Inc. Includes two other fanciful poems.

Hoppity

PAGE 49

PRE-READING PREPARATION

Background for the Selection

This poem by A. A. Milne is taken from his collection for young children entitled *When We Were Very Young.* Since *Christopher* and *Robin* are not names usually known by American children, it is important that they realize that Christopher Robin in this poem is a little boy, the son of the poet. (Some children may know Christopher Robin from *Winnie-the-Pooh*.) In this poem, there is nothing particularly British; but in some of the other poems, there are British characteristics. The point here is merely that Christopher Robin, like many other children, likes to skip and hop rather than walk sedately along the street.

Elements of Literature

The rhythm of a poem can take many forms, but it is used to best advantage when rhythm and idea are compatible and synchronized. "Hoppity" is an unusually fine example of this, and the literary qualities that will be emphasized are:
1. the rhythm of the poem fits the idea.
2. the mood of the poem can be sensed from certain words.

Introducing the Selection

1. Ask children if they have ever had to walk with younger brothers or sisters when shopping or visiting. If so, ask them what the children did. They will probably tell you that their young brothers and sisters kept hopping and skipping and investigating everything along the route.
2. Then tell pupils that in the poem you are going to read to them, the little boy, whose name is Christopher Robin, likes to go hopping and skipping along, too.
3. Ask pupils to open their books to page 49 and look at the picture. Let them talk about Christopher Robin and the way he is dressed. Point out that he lived in England a long time ago.
4. Read the poem aloud, asking children to listen and see if they can tell why Christopher Robin must hop. Practice reading this

poem aloud before you read it to the class so that you can give the poem a hopping rhythm. For example, stop after the second *hoppity*, then say the next two *hoppitys* and the *hop* in one breath. Drop your voice with finality on the *hop*.

POST-READING EXTENSION

Exploring the Selection

Questions to ask
1. Check the pupils' listening abilities by asking who Christopher Robin is. (He is a boy.) What does he do? (He goes hoppity.)
2. Why does Christopher Robin need to hop? (He couldn't go anywhere if he didn't hop.)
3. Who do you think is with him? (The poem says "I" and could be his father or another older person.)
4. How do you think Christopher Robin feels as he goes hopping along? (Probably happy, cheerful, glad, though you should accept any reasonable answer from the children.)
5. Where do you think Christopher Robin goes when he is hopping? (Answers will vary according to the child's own experiences.)

Interpreting Literature

Rhythm
1. The rhythm in this poem is very pronounced, and your reading has given it a hopping movement. Ask children to notice how the rhythm of the *hoppity's* makes a person feel like hopping. Compare the word *hoppity* with *hopping* to note the difference in rhythm, and help pupils sense that the former gives the actual "hopping" feeling, while the latter only tells what is being done.

Mood
2. The mood of the poem is gay, light, and rather sympathetic. Let children say *hoppity* several times, then ask them whether they think *hoppity* hopping is happy or sad. (Accept their answers, but try to get them to tell their reasons.) Then point out the lines, "Poor little Christopher / Couldn't go anywhere . . . ," and see if they catch the humor, sympathy, and hint of resignation there. (They may see this only as a realistic explanation; to children, the reason given for hopping is most sensible. But the light-hearted feeling ought to be sensed and recognized.) Ask the children if they can tell how someone feels by the way he walks. Then have a child demonstrate and let others guess how he feels.

Developing Language Skills

Vocabulary development
1. The words in this poem should all be within the child's grasp, but extend his vocabulary by discussing other words that describe locomotion, such as: *walk, run, jump, dart, skip,* and so on.

Interpretive activities
2. Have several children, individually, demonstrate the way they think Christopher Robin hopped along. They may choose a

partner to be "I" if they wish. Then ask the pupils to say the poem with you, paying attention to the number of *hoppity's* and to the rhythm. Then ask if someone can say the *hoppity's* a different way to show a different kind of hopping. After this, you might play the recording of this poem from *Poetry Time* (Chicago: Scott, Foresman and Company) in which Mrs. May Hill Arbuthnot recites the poem. Children could decide the way they like it best, though not all will agree.

Research activities
3. Ask children to watch preschoolers to see if they act like Christopher Robin, and then report to the class later about it.

Books to read
4. Have copies of Milne's poetry books, *When We Were Very Young*, from which "Hoppity" is taken, and *Now We Are Six* for children to look at and for you to use in reading to them. Another Milne poem with a decided rhythm is "Busy." Mother Goose rhymes with a special rhythmic quality include "Tom, Tom, the Piper's Son," "Wee Willie Winkie," or "Hush-a-Bye, Baby," which has a swinging (6/8) rhythm.

Audio-visual aids
5. The following audio-visual aids are recommended for use with this selection:

Hoppity Pop. 3-minute color film. National Film Board of Canada. Made by Norman McLaren, this film shows colors and shapes moving to caliope music.

Hoppy, the Rabbit. Color filmstrip. Jam Handy School Service. Shows the way a rabbit hops.

Pet Rabbit, in the set *Pets.* Record and study print. Society for Visual Education, Inc. Includes a large 18″ × 13″ rabbit picture.

My Bunny. Color filmstrip. Eye Gate House, Inc.

A Tree Is Nice

PRE-READING PREPARATION

Background for the Selection

All of the original text from the book *A Tree Is Nice* by Janice May Udry is reproduced for the children. Marc Simont, who did the illustrations, was given the Caldecott Award for this book in 1957. The story takes a somewhat different approach from the usual children's book, because here trees are viewed as a useful, aesthetic part of our environment. They are not regarded as scientific plants or as personified trees (like Hans Christian Andersen's "The Fir Tree"), or as symbolic influences on people (like *Tree in the Trail* by Holling C. Holling). In *A Tree Is Nice*, the approach implies that man appreciates and uses the trees that are here, or he plants new ones to serve his purpose. Trees are also nice for animals and houses. The words that tell the theme of the story—"a tree is nice"—are repeated at intervals throughout the selection, and children should grasp the theme without any difficulty.

Elements of Literature

As indicated, this story is more an emotional appreciation of trees than it is a story about a specific tree or a factual, nonfictional account. Thus, the literary qualities of the selection do not deal with sequence or pattern so much as they reflect style. Three aspects have been selected for attention:
1. the cadence resulting from repetition.
2. the movement created by the action words.
3. the shifting point of view.

Introducing the Selection

1. Call attention to any trees that can be seen from the schoolroom windows. If you think your children may be unfamiliar with trees, take them for a walk in the vicinity of the school or in a park. Have them note the tree's characteristics, such as size, shape, trunk and branches, leaves, and seeds. If there are no trees near the school, collect pictures of various types of trees to use as an introduction. You may wish to include both evergreen and

deciduous trees, and trees from various parts of the country (including palm trees), to show the variety.

2. If children have had experience with trees, ask them if they have a favorite tree and let them talk about it, or you might tell of your own experiences with trees as a child.

3. Direct the children to open their books to the page on which the story begins. You may wish to write the number on the chalkboard so the children can match it with the one in the book.

4. Let the children leaf through the pages of the story before you read it. Encourage spontaneous discussion as children look at the pictures. Once the children have looked through the pictures, they will more readily concentrate on each page that you read.

5. Explain to the children that the story tells many different ways that trees are nice for children and others. Ask them to see how many ideas they can remember after they have heard the story.

6. Ask the children to turn to the first page of the story and look at the picture while you read what the story says. Continue without interruption through the story, having children turn pages when you do. (With immature groups, you may need to read and discuss the story page-by-page, but it would be better if you could read the story as a whole, then have the discussion.)

POST-READING EXTENSION

Exploring the Selection

Sharing Time   Have pupils turn to the Sharing Time page. Read each question and let the children turn back to the story as they formulate their answers.

1. This summary question would include the information given on the actual pages (includes play, walk, roll, build playhouses, pile up and have a bonfire, climb, sit and think, play pirate ship, pick apples, hang a swing or basket of flowers, and lean a hoe against). You might make a list on the chalkboard as ideas are given, then let children refer to their books to add other information until the list is complete.

2. In addition to the play already discussed, children should also tell that trees help cows by shading them; that cats can get away from dogs by climbing up trees; that birds can build their nests in trees, and the like.

3. The story gives an answer, but children who have planted trees may have additional specific information.

4. Any reasonable answer is acceptable here. Children may talk about fruits and nuts, squirrels and birds, pine cones and Christmas trees, lumber and plywood, depending on the section of the country. You may stimulate some ideas if children seem to "draw a blank" here.

The discussion about trees might be followed by other questions such as:

1. Where does the story say that trees grow? (Beside the rivers, down the valleys, up on the hills.) Where else do trees grow? (Along the street, in parks, in people's yards, and so on.)
2. Why would people plant a tree after they have seen one planted? (Because they would see how nice a tree can be.)
3. Have you ever planted a tree? Tell us about it. (If you have an Arbor Day at your school, you can give some preparation for the occasion now.)
4. What can we do to take care of trees? (Children may cite such things as not pulling up or stamping on young trees, not tearing off bark, and watering trees when they need it.)

Interpreting Literature

Cadence 1. The story has a slow, easy cadence due in part to the repetition of the phrase, "A tree is nice," and in part to the number of compound sentences. Children can listen or look for the phrase "A tree is nice," and see how many times it is repeated in the story. You could ask the children how the story makes them feel. (Their answers might include: quiet, slow, busy, and such, but probably not noisy, fast, or funny.) Try to contrast the style of this selection with a quick, choppy, fast selection that the children know—perhaps a nursery rhyme like "To market, to market"—and call attention to the difference in feeling.

Movement 2. The movement in the story is pushed along by the many action words. You could reread a page at a time and ask the children to notice the words that tell what trees and people do. For example, the first page tells that trees "fill up," "go," and "live." You might want to call attention to the personification (attributing human qualities to nonhuman things) of the trees *going* beside the rivers. This is not too difficult for children to understand because they accept the make-believe easily.

Several parts of the story contain action verbs relating to people. (They walk, roll in leaves, build leaf houses, pile up leaves, and have a bonfire. They climb, look, sit and think, play pirate ship. They dig, put in trees, pour water and dirt, hang up the shovel, and the like.) All of the action verbs help to move the story along.

Point of view 3. While you would not use the term "point of view" with the children at this level, you can help them recognize that different people are talking or being talked to in the story. You might begin by asking children if they can identify the *we* on the fourth page and on the next three pages. (Here the author includes himself with the reader.) The story then switches to *you*—"to lean your hoe while you rest." At the end of the story, the author moves to other people. ("They wish they had one, . . .") Not all children will grasp this idea the first time it is presented, but a discussion in connection with this story ought to help them understand that different people are mentioned.

Developing Language Skills

Vocabulary development 1. Although children may be familiar with trees, they may not know the words *trunk* and *limb*. Several other words in the story may also need definition through explanation or illustration. Here are some to consider:

trunk: the main stem of a tree, as distinct from the branches and roots

limb: large branch

pirate: a robber on the sea

lean: set or put up in a slanting position

hoe: a tool with a small blade set across the end of a long handle, used for loosening the soil or cutting weeds

shovel: a tool with a broad scoop, used to lift and throw loose matter

It would be a good idea to show a real or toy hoe and shovel, for some children may not know these tools and their names. Another concept that may not be clear is how to "build a playhouse" out of leaves. Explain that the children in the story simply take some of the leaves out of the center of the pile, and make small ridges to show where the walls of the house are. Openings are left for the doors. Playing "pirate ship" may also need more explanation, for children will need to visualize the limbs of trees as ships from which one can see the distant horizons. While the story does not mention a tree house, some child may have had experience with a platform or an actual shelter that was built in the branches of a tree, and this concept can be added to those already learned.

Interpretive activities 2. Have children draw a picture to show their favorite part of the story or their favorite activity connected with trees.

Research activities 3. Ask children to collect pictures of trees for a bulletin board display. Arrange the pictures on the bulletin board by types of trees. Label those that can be identified.

For a related art activity, children could collect various leaves, press them flat between newspapers, and use them like a stencil to make spatter designs. The leaf is placed on the paper, and poster paint is brushed over a screen held a few inches above the design. A toothbrush or other stiff brush is best. Designs can include several leaves for variation, and two colors can be spattered on the same page. These designs make good covers for booklets as well as pictures to display.

Books to read 4. Have available a copy of the book *A Tree Is Nice* by Janice May Udry. Since the size of this book is different from that of the textbook, children can compare the two and discuss differences. Other books related to this selection include *Lookout for the Forest* by Glenn O. Blough (especially the parts concerning the use of trees), *Ten Big Farms* by Dahlov Ipcar (the part about fruit trees), and *I Found a Leaf* by Sharon Lerner.

Audio-visual aids 5. The following audio-visual aids are recommended for use with this selection:

A Tree Is Nice.   Color and sound filmstrip. Weston Woods Studios.

The Tree.   Color filmstrip. Churchill Films. Shows the importance of trees for living things.

Talk About Trees, in the set *A Child's World of Poetry — Group 2.* Record and color study print. Society for Visual Education, Inc. Includes an 18″ × 13″ picture and related poems.

Clouds

PAGE 64

PRE-READING PREPARATION

Background for the Selection

This poem by Dorothy Aldis is taken from her collection entitled *All Together: A Child's Treasury of Verses.* Mrs. Aldis has written many poems for young children, and she consistently presents ideas from a child's point of view, directly and simply, with regular rhythm and rhyme schemes. She meets children at their own level, and they respond. Mrs. Aldis presents clear images, a new way of looking at ordinary things, and a surprise at the end. Young children wonder about things they see around them, and this poem catches them wondering if clouds taste as good as they look.

Elements of Literature

Although this poem is about the ordinary topic of clouds, its appeal lies both in the image it creates, and in its sound. These two aspects will be discussed with the children after the poem has been read:
1. the visual image created by the idea of the poem.
2. the alliteration and other sounds in the poem.

Introducing the Selection

1. Ask pupils if they ever lie on their backs outdoors in the grass and watch the clouds move across the sky. Let different children tell about their experiences. Or look out of the schoolroom window and see if there are any clouds in the sky.
2. Discuss various types of clouds without using the specific terminology, but recall with children the black, thick, thunder clouds; the thin, wispy, high clouds; the big, fluffy, cottony clouds; and so on. If you have some good colored pictures of different cloud types, let children have a chance to see them and talk about them.
3. Ask the pupils if they ever try to figure out what the clouds look like, such as: sheep, cars, horses, or wild geese.
4. Ask the children to open their books to page 64 and to look at the picture. Have volunteers tell what the child might be thinking about. After the children have made suggestions, tell them you will read the poem and they can see if they were correct.

POST-READING EXTENSION

Exploring the Selection

Questions to ask 1. Check with the children to see if their suggestions about the child were correct. (The answer will depend on what they have suggested.) If they did not guess correctly, ask what the child in the poem wanted to do. (Scoop up clouds and have them cooked to see if they taste good.)

2. Ask pupils how the child was going to get the clouds. (With a spoon as tall as the sky.)

3. Then ask who the "I" in the poem is. (While the author writes in the first person, she is actually putting herself in a child's place, and therefore it is a child who is talking.)

4. What do you think clouds would taste like? (You may need to stimulate some answers with suggestions like soft ice cream, white cotton candy, or whipped cream. See if children relate the color and texture of clouds to the counterparts suggested.)

Interpreting Literature

Imagery 1. Poetry is a combination of subject, form, and feeling. This poem emphasizes a single idea and creates a sensory image that is within the comprehension of the children. Note the size of the spoon and ask children how big (tall) the spoon would need to be. While they will not recognize the simile, "as tall as the sky," they will recognize that the spoon must be tall—tall enough to reach up and scoop the clouds.

Sounds 2. Note how the beginning sounds for s—*spoon, sky, slip-sliding*, and *see*—keep the poem moving easily along. Note, too, the way the smooth turning of the words in the mouth makes one feel as if he is almost tasting the clouds. While you will not use with the children the term *alliteration*, which is the repetition of the same first sound in a group of words or line of poetry, you can ask them to listen for sounds that are repeated and to name the words that begin with the same sound or with a sound you designate. If necessary, reread the poem until all the words beginning with s have been named. (Some children might also notice the sounds for s in *clouds, as,* and *tasted*.)

Developing Language Skills

Vocabulary development 1. One word in the poem that may be unfamiliar to the children is:

cook: a person who prepares food by using heat

The term may need further explanation to distinguish *cook* from *Mother*, but if there is a school cafeteria or restaurant nearby, you can refer to the cooks there.

Children might also name other words beginning with *s*, or they might think of all the "food words" they can.

2. Children might like to pantomime the poem, pretending to reach for the clouds, bring them down, give them to cook, then eat them. You might have two or three children say the poem with you as some of the others pantomime. Individual children who know the poem by now can say it alone.

3. Children might ask older brothers or sisters how clouds are formed, or the class might invite an older child to come and tell how clouds are formed. Children could also find pictures of clouds in magazines and make a collection of those that look good enough to eat.

4. Have available a copy of *All Together: A Child's Treasury of Verse* by Dorothy Aldis, for it contains this poem and a selected group from her other books of poetry for children. You might also wish to get *The Storm Book* by Charlotte Zolotow, for it describes other kinds of clouds, or *The Little House* by Virginia Lee Burton, whose pictures include some billowy clouds.

5. The following audio-visual aids are recommended for use with this selection:

Clouds. 10-minute color film. Bailey-Film Associates. Presents a variety of observations on clouds.

Familiar Cloud Forms, in the *Basic Science Series* set. Color study print. Society for Visual Education, Inc. Contains large 18″ × 13″ pictures of various clouds, including fog.

Spring Rain

PAGE 65

PRE-READING PREPARATION

Background for the Selection

Marchette Chute has written several books of poetry for children. This poem is taken from her book entitled *Rhymes About the City*, though the locale of the poem could be almost anywhere. The sudden coming of a thunderstorm catches the person in the poem without his rain gear. This is a predicament most people have faced, but not, perhaps, with the glee described in the second verse. The child's point of view is obvious here, for most adults get annoyed when good clothes get wet in a sudden shower.

Elements of Literature

The impact of this poem is humorous and gay and rather carefree. Three aspects of the poem contribute to its total impression, and they will be selected for discussion with the children after the poem has been read:
1. the sound created by the use of short, clipped words.
2. the sharp, staccato accent.
3. the repetition and form of the poem.

Introducing the Selection

1. Ask the children if they have ever been caught in the rain without a raincoat or an umbrella. Let them tell what happened. Or show them a picture of someone who is caught getting wet in a downpour. Point out the difference between being caught unexpectedly and just standing outside and purposely getting wet in a summer shower.
2. Tell the children that this poem is about someone who gets caught in the rain. Ask them to listen to find out whether or not the person liked it.
3. Then ask pupils to open their books to page 65 and look at the picture. This gives them more information regarding the mood of the poem. Read the poem aloud as the children have their books open and can see the picture.

boy in picture
doesn't look
very wet

POST-READING EXTENSION

Exploring the Selection

Questions to ask 1. Ask the children how the person in the poem feels about getting wet. (They might say the person is glad or happy or that he likes it.) Try to get children to figure out what gives them this idea. (The sound of the poem plus the line, "But this is even better.")

2. Who is the "I" in the poem? (Since nothing has been said about the author, the children might answer, "a boy" or "a girl" or "a child." They might give reasons for their choice.)

3. What happened to the person in the poem? (He got caught in the rain without a raincoat or hat.)

4. How can you keep from getting caught in the rain yourself? (Check the weather and take rain gear with you if necessary.)

Interpreting Literature

Sounds 1. The pace and mood of this poem are created in part by the sound of the short, clipped words. Note the number of one-syllable words that help make for quick reading. Reread the poem and ask children which words make the poem sound funny and fast. (They may say *quicker* and *slicker* or *wetter* and *better*, for these two-syllable words tend to break the pattern formed by the one-syllable words.) Notice, too, that many of the vowel sounds are short rather than long, which adds to the crispness of the poem.

Accent 2. The decided accent or beat of this poem is due to the choice of words and the way they are put together. The important words and parts of words receive the accent. (The *storm* came *up* so *very quick*.) Ask children to tap out the rhythm on their knees or to clap softly as you read the poem. Exaggerate the accent somewhat.

Form 3. Note the many lines that include some repetition: the "quick—quicker" and "wet—wetter" parts, the words "I should have brought," and "My _____ is wet," and the repetition of "I" as the first word in many of the lines. Have children point out these repetitive parts and notice how these emphasize the idea.

Note also that the rhyme scheme is actually *a b c b*, but with the *quick—quicker* and *wet—wetter* there is an additional touch that contributes to the humor of the poem.

All the lines except the last one are simple sentences. The shift to the compound sentence in the last two lines changes the pace of the poem and gives a little surprise ending to it. All of this may not be apparent to the children, but they should catch the idea and respond to the fun in the poem.

Developing Language Skills

Vocabulary development 1. Two words likely to need definition in this poem are:

slicker: a long, loose, waterproof coat
river: a large stream of water

Let children name other articles of rainwear, like *rubbers, over-shoes,* and *umbrellas.* Then have them name other forms of precipitation like *snow, hail, sleet,* and other words associated with weather, such as *thunder, lightning, fog, drizzle, rainbow,* and *wind.* On the chalkboard, you might list these words in groups related to a topic. Then use these words to make up a group poem about the weather.

Interpretive activities 2. Encourage children to say the poem with you as you read and reread it. Then try the group alone, without your help. When they seem to know it, let different children take different lines, and the others say the rest. You could review all the "rain poems" children know and talk about the phrases or words that paint good pictures. If you have a tape recorder, let individuals and groups record a related series of poems, then play back the tape as a program. (The closed loop, cartridge recorders are very simple to operate, and the tapes can be reused.)

Research activities 3. If it is a rainy day when you use this poem, ask several children to bring their raincoats to the front of the room and compare the waterproof material in them. Have a committee of children find out the school rules about sudden storms.

Books to read 4. Get a copy of Marchette Chute's *Rhymes About the City,* where this poem is found. Some of her other collections of poetry for children are: *Around and About* and *Rhymes About Ourselves. The Storm Book* by Charlotte Zolotow, which the children may already have seen, and *Rain Drop Splash* by Alvin Tresselt are good picture books on the topic.

Audio-visual aids 5. The following audio-visual aids are recommended for use with this selection:
Rain Shower. 15-minute color film. Churchill Films. Shows the rhythm and beat of the rain.
Sun Up by Alvin Tresselt. Color and sound filmstrip. Weston Woods Studios. Shows a thunderstorm coming and going.
A Walk in the Rain, in the *Learning About the Seasons* series. Color and sound filmstrip. Society for Visual Education, Inc. Shows how the spring rain helps things to grow.
Spring. 9-minute color film. Sterling Educational Films.

One Was Johnny

PAGES 66–78

PRE-READING PREPARATION

Background for the Selection

This simple counting story is a reproduction of the book *One Was Johnny* by Maurice Sendak. The numbers go up from one to ten and then go back down to one. The text is composed almost entirely of couplets (two-line verses), and for each number there is a fanciful or humorous idea. *One Was Johnny* is a tiny book, [and the reproductions in the text show double-page spreads.] (61)

with one number per page, the text usually shows two. 53

The author-artist received the Caldecott Award in 1964 for the illustrations in *Where the Wild Things Are*. In 1970, he was given the Hans Christian Andersen Awards Illustrator's Medal, the highest international honor to an illustrator of children's books. Maurice Sendak has a real feeling for children and their fun, and his ideas and pictorial interpretations are understood and loved by children. If you have a chance to see the film *The Lively Art of Picture Books* (Weston Woods Studios), you will see and hear Sendak state his own philosophy concerning illustrating for children. He is one of three illustrators interviewed in the film.

Elements of Literature

The appeal of this selection is based on several factors combined to achieve an integrated effect. The story pattern and the humor are the principal elements of appeal; therefore, the two literary understandings that will be emphasized here are:
1. the accumulative story pattern.
2. the humor, both of situation and of fanciful idea.

Introducing the Selection

1. Ask how many children can count to ten. First let the class count in unison, then let individual children count.
2. Ask if anyone knows the Mother Goose rhyme of "One, two, three, four, five, / I caught a hare alive." If no one does, read or recite it for the class. (The rest of the rhyme is: "Six, seven, eight, nine, ten, / I let her go again.") Let the children contribute other counting-out poems.

3. If no one suggests "One, two, buckle my shoe," ask if anyone knows it. If they don't, recite or read it to them. Point out that every two lines rhyme, so the words are easy to learn. Say the rhyme again and let them say it with you.

4. Tell the children that their story for today is a counting rhyme, too.

5. Ask children to open their books to the first page of the story. (Write the page number on the chalkboard for the children to match.) Note that there are two pictures on most of the pages. Explain that these are taken from the original little book and that *where* each picture is actually two facing pages. Have the children follow the numbers and the pictures as you read. Point to each number as you say it, and then read the accompanying sentence.

POST-READING EXTENSION

Sharing Time

Exploring the Selection

Ask the children to turn to the Sharing Time page after the story. Then take each of the questions in order.

1. Probably one child cannot name all the animals, but let several try. (The visitors, in order, are: rat, cat, dog, turtle, monkey, blackbird, tiger, and robber.)

2. Answers will vary, and accept any part the child chooses. See if he can tell why he thinks that part is funny. Each child can draw a picture for the funny part later when he has time, or you can give the whole class time to draw whenever you wish.

3. Children will realize Johnny's bewilderment at such a full house, and they may say he didn't know what to do. Some may think he was angry at having his solitude invaded; others may think he felt cramped with so many around. Accept only reasonable answers that children can justify.

4. Make sure the children understand the meaning of *clever*. Most pupils will recognize the cleverness of Johnny's "threat" to eat everyone if they weren't gone by the time he finished counting. Some might also say that Johnny was clever in that he was able to avoid a confrontation with the whole group, and still get them out of his house.

5. Accept any reasonable answer that includes an attempt to meet the problem.

Additional questions if time permits

Following are some supplementary questions you might wish to ask about the selection:

1. Which visitors acted the way you would expect and which seemed make-believe? (Answers may vary; however, the rat, cat, turtle, blackbird, and robber acted more true to life than the dog, the monkey, and the tiger when both comings and goings are taken into consideration.)

73

2. Why do you think Johnny let them all come in? (He was too busy reading to notice; he liked company, especially animals; he thought they might go away when they saw the others that were already there; he was too surprised to do anything at first. Accept any reasonable answer.)
3. What would have happened if the visitors had not left? (Johnny said he would eat them, but do you really think he would?)
4. How did Johnny act when each one came in? (Have the children look at Johnny in the pictures. Each picture would need to be interpreted, but Johnny's expressions are exaggerated enough to do so with ease. For example: **1** shows Johnny self-satisfied; **2**, surprised; **3**, upset; **4**, bewildered; **5**, wondering; **6**, resigned; **7**, howling; **8**, astonished; **9**, exasperated; **10**, puzzled; **9**, smug; **8**, gleeful; **7**, gay and airy; **6**, stern; **5**, pleased; **4**, questioning; **3**, afraid; **2**, irritated; **1**, proud and happy; and at the end, joyous. While children will not use these words or their synonyms, they should be able to interpret the expressions to give the idea of Johnny's feelings.)

Interpreting Literature

Story pattern 1. Some folktales and modern make-believe stories have an accumulative story pattern, just as this story does. The pattern is just what the word implies—the story accumulates as it goes along, just as Johnny accumulated a houseful of visitors. Two well-known accumulative old tales are *The House That Jack Built* and *The Old Woman and Her Pig*. In both of these, however, the parts accumulated are repeated in the story, whereas in Johnny's case, each is added individually. For example in *The House That Jack Built*, the parts about the malt, rat, cat, and so on, are repeated each time a new one is added.

The story about Johnny is much simpler and provides less repetition. Explain the idea of adding characters as the story moves forward and see if the children can name the events in the order in which they occur in the story. You might list the events on the chalkboard.

Humor 2. Humor for young children is often based upon a surprise (including a physical situation like falling down, or upon an unexpected turn of events). The humor is also often based on exaggeration of one kind or another. This story contains both types of humor. The rat surprises Johnny and enters from an unexpected angle; the cat follows and looks ruefully at the rat, but does sit down beside him. The cat's expressions are not lost on the children, nor is the supercilious air of the dog that sits. Each picture and caption contains much humor, and children will want to point out each and discuss it. The antics of the monkey are unusually appealing, and you might ask children whether or not real monkeys could do what this one does.

Developing Language Skills

Vocabulary development 1. The language in this story is easy; however, a few words might need discussion or clarification:

chased:	ran after to catch
puzzle:	a hard problem
empty:	with nothing in it
pale:	without much color; whitish
Havana:	the capital city of Cuba
pounced:	jumped suddenly and seized

Interpretive activities 2. This story lends itself well to dramatization since the verbs are so descriptive and the pictures so explicit. Ask for volunteers for each character to play the story through. Let others discuss how the presentation could be improved. Then ask for volunteers from among those who have not yet had a turn. If necessary, play the story a third time until each child has had a chance to participate. The rest of the class can be the audience with appropriate responsibilities. Ask children to note especially anyone who interpreted his character in keeping with the story.

This is also a good story to use for making a class mural, with parts assigned to individuals or to pairs to work at odd moments or during an assigned period. You might write the appropriate text on the section of the paper allotted to that part.

Research activities 3. Some children may be interested in finding out more about turtles, monkeys, and blackbirds. They might look at books, ask parents or older brothers and sisters, and report back to the class.

Books to read 4. Have a copy of Maurice Sendak's *One Was Johnny* on the reading table along with other counting books like *3 X 3 Three by Three*, by James Kruss; *Jeanne-Marie Counts Her Sheep* by Françoise; *1 Is One* by Tasha Tudor; and *One Step, Two* by Charlotte Zolotow. You might want to have a copy of *Where the Wild Things Are*, also by Maurice Sendak, for the children to enjoy. They could contrast the illustrations with those in *One Was Johnny*, noting the differences in size, expression, action, and humor.

Audio-visual aids 5. The following audio-visual aids are recommended for use with this selection:

Alphabet and Counting Songs. Record. Eye Gate House, Inc.
Brown Cow Farm. Color and sound filmstrip. Weston Woods Studios.

Star Light, Star Bright

PAGE 79

PRE-READING PREPARATION

Background for the Selection

This traditional rhyme has come down through oral means, and often children chant the verse as they see the first star of evening. It is interesting to note how generations pass on their sayings and verses to future generations. Children at play exchange rope-jumping rhymes, ways of counting out for "It," and singing games. Until someone records these rhymes, they exist only in oral form, just as folktales do. The rhymes may assume a local flavor, as children change and revise and add their own phrases.

The poem "Star Light, Star Bright" has universal appeal, for what child has watched the stars come out, one by one, and not wondered what they are, how they got into the sky, and how they stay up there. This poem is one of the Mother Goose charms which, in spite of scientific advances in knowledge about the universe, is still interesting to children today.

Elements of Literature

This rhyme contains lyrical, or singing, qualities not found in some of the Mother Goose rhymes, for its combination of sound and idea make it truly poetic. These two qualities will be considered in the discussion that follows:

1. the sounds as they combine to create a mood.
2. the appeal to the child's imagination.

Introducing the Selection

1. Ask pupils if they have ever stood outside and watched the stars come out, one by one, first here, then there. For city children, this is sometimes difficult, because city lights shut out the stars, except perhaps in a big city park. However, children who have had this experience will want to' tell about it. Ask the children to tell what they think of when they see the stars hanging up there all by themselves. In case you do not get a response from children, tell them of your own experiences in watching stars come out at night.

2. Then inquire whether or not the pupils have ever wished at a wishing well or a fountain or on a chicken's wishbone. Let them tell about it and report whether or not their wishes came true.

3. Now direct the children to open their books to page 79 and look at the picture. What could the child in the picture be thinking? After children make several suggestions, let them know that the poem tells what the child is saying. Ask them to listen and find out what the child *is* saying as you read the poem. (The rhyme may be familiar to some of the children, so be prepared for their chiming in with you.)

POST-READING EXTENSION

Exploring the Selection

Questions to ask
1. After you finish reading, ask pupils whether or not they were correct in their guesses as to what the child was saying. (She was making a wish on a star.)

2. What in the poem makes you think she wants her wish very much? (The repetition of "I wish I may, I wish I might.")

3. Why do you suppose she wishes on the *first* star? (Children can conjecture about the importance of seeing the *first* star. Accept any reasonable answer.)

4. What do you think she is wishing for? (Children's answers will probably reflect what they would like themselves.)

5. Have you ever wished on a star? Did you use this rhyme? What happened? (Let them tell their experiences.)

6. What would you wish for tonight if you saw a star? (Answers will vary.)

7. Do you think wishes on a star will really come true? (Try to help children realize the fun without being too disappointed when wishes are not fulfilled.)

Interpreting Literature

Sounds
1. The light, bright mood of this poem is created in part by the use of several long vowel sounds—the *i*'s and *a*'s. Note the number of words containing these sounds, and ask the children to listen to them as you read the poem again. (*Light, bright, I, tonight, may, might, tonight.*) Call attention to the way these long vowel sounds slow down the speed and create a questioning attitude. Compare, if you wish, with the short vowel sounds in "Spring Rain" and note how the pace and mood are affected in each by the sounds for the vowels. Ask children how the words "star light, star bright" make them feel. (Perhaps they will catch the light, airy feeling that the poem conveys.) Note also how the repetition and rhythm of sounds—the *star*, and the *wish*—both give emphasis to

the wish in a wistful rather than insistent manner. You might also compare the sounds in this poem with those in "Firefly."

Appeal to imagination 2. The idea of using a star to wish upon can set the child's imagination soaring. Children are very much aware of their world and are trying to find out about it. Children also create imaginary worlds of their own; and since stars are remote physically, they are "proper stuff" for imaginary worlds. While today's child has watched the moon explorations as a matter of fact, he still can wonder as he sees the heavenly bodies at night. Ask the children why they think people began wishing on stars and see if they connect this to the lack of knowledge about the universe. Accept any reasonable answer, but stimulate children to try to give some suggestions. They could also suggest other objects that might be good to use when making a wish.

Developing Language Skills

Vocabulary development 1. The words in this poem are within the vocabulary of most children of this age. So use the opportunity to extend their vocabularies by discussing related topics. Children may talk of the moon explorations, other planets might be named, constellations like the Big and Little Dippers might be mentioned, and children could be instructed to look at night for the Big Dipper. Spontaneous oral discussion promotes vocabulary development if you take the opportunity to introduce new words to the class.

Interpretive activities 2. This poem is easy to learn because of the simple idea and the repetition. Say the poem all together, then let one group say the first two lines and the other group say the last two. Individual children may wish to recite it, and let a few do so. You might suggest that they say it at home for their parents or older brothers and sisters. They may also wish to make illustrations for the bulletin board, and you could make another page for your Big Book on tagboard.

Research activities 3. Suggest that the class collect poems about night and the universe. Some may know "The Moon's the North Wind's Cooky" and other poems to start. This can become an ongoing activity and carry through into succeeding books.

Pupils might also make a collection of sidewalk rhymes and ditties that all children seem to know. These could be made into a group book and illustrated.

Books to read 4. Have available Mother Goose books that contain this poem. Try especially to get *The Rooster Crows* by Maud and Miska Petersham and let the children see their lovely illustration for this poem. Also note the contemporary rope-skipping rhymes and the finger-plays in this collection. Another contemporary book of rhymes is *The American Mother Goose* by Ray Wood.

(WITHIN EACH MAJOR CATEGORY, ITEMS ARE
ARRANGED ALPHABETICALLY. PAGE NUMBERS
REFER TO TEACHER'S EDITION ONLY.)

Appreciation and Understanding of Literature

Accent: 57, 70

Accumulative story pattern: 74

Action words: 63

Alliteration: 50–51, 67

Cadence: 50, 53, 57, 63

Ending: 44, 56, 70

Figure of speech: 32

Folktale pattern: 45, 47

Humor: 29, 74

Illustrations: 29

Imagery: 40, 53, 67

Metaphor: 32

Mood: 36–37, 59, 77–78

Moral: 47

Narrative poetry: 38

Nonsense words: 29

Personification: 63

Poetry: 35, 36, 55

Point of view: 63–64

Repetition: 36, 47, 63, 70, 77–78

Rhyme: 32, 40, 43, 50, 51, 53, 57

Rhyme scheme: 42, 43, 57, 70

Rhythm: 36–37, 40, 43, 50, 53, 59, 70, 77–78

Simile: 67

Sounds of words: 29, 40, 53, 67, 70, 77–78

Vocabulary Development

Extending vocabulary through discussion: 29–30, 37, 40–41, 44, 48, 51, 57, 59, 64, 67, 71, 75, 78

Learning about connotation: 53–54

Learning word meanings: 33, 39, 43, 51, 57, 64, 67, 70, 75

Working with action words: 59

Working with words that rhyme: 41

Oral and Listening Skills

Conducting choral reading: 33, 57, 71, 78

Dramatizing a story: 41, 48, 51, 54, 59–60, 68, 75

Giving an oral report: 33, 41

Making up a group poem: 71

Reciting a poem: 30, 33, 37, 44, 51, 57, 68, 71, 78

Art Activities

Doing creative drawing: 41

Illustrating a poem: 30, 37, 44, 54, 57, 78

Illustrating a story: 64

Making a mural: 75

Making spatter designs: 64

Starting a loose-leaf scrapbook: 57, 78

Research Activities

Acquiring information from other sources: 30, 33, 37, 44, 51, 60, 68, 71, 75

Collecting pictures, games, stories, or poems: 37, 41, 48, 57, 64, 68, 78

Making a report: 37, 60, 75

Helen Huus
Professor of Education
University of Missouri–Kansas City

Robert J. Whitehead
Professor of Education
Sacramento State College

Program Director
Henry A. Bamman
Professor of Education
Sacramento State College

Field Educational Publications, Incorporated

A Subsidiary of Field Enterprises, Incorporated
San Francisco   Addison, Ill.   Berkeley Heights, N.J.   Atlanta   Dallas

Apple Trees

Field Literature Program

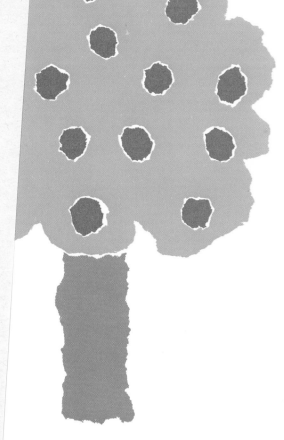

Books you <u>can</u> judge by their covers

Field Literature Program

...nly literature of the finest quality
...found in the Field Literature Pro-
...am. This completely new K-6 pro-
...am combines appealing content
...d extensive use of original illus-
...tions to stimulate students' de-
...e to read for pleasure.
...Selections are well balanced be-
...een poetry and prose, fiction and
...n-fiction, humor, fantasy, adven-
...e and biography. Each selection
...of equal interest to both boys
...girls.

Standard Book Number 514–01201–3

Acknowledgments

The order of acknowledgments follows the sequence of selections in the Table of Contents.

Grateful acknowledgment is made to the following sources for permission to reprint copyrighted material:

Illustrations from "Hey Diddle Diddle" by Randolph Caldecott, used by permission of Frederick Warne & Co., Inc.

"Firefly," from *Under the Tree* by Elizabeth Madox Roberts. Copyright 1922 by B. W. Huebsch, Inc., renewed 1950 by Ivor S. Roberts. Reprinted by permission of The Viking Press, Inc.

"One Is Good but Two Are Better," abridged and reprinted by permission of the publisher, The Vanguard Press, from *One Is Good but Two Are Better* by Louis Slobodkin. Illustrations by the author. Copyright, 1956, by Louis Slobodkin.

"Tommy," from *Bronzeville Boys and Girls* by Gwendolyn Brooks. Copyright © 1956 by Gwendolyn Brooks Blakely. Reprinted with permission of Harper & Row, Publishers.

"The Little Red Hen and the Grain of Wheat," reprinted by permission of G. P. Putnam's Sons from *Chimney Corner Stories* by Veronica S. Hutchinson. Copyright 1925 by Minton, Balch & Co.

Illustration of "Jack and Jill," from *Mother Goose* by Kate Greenaway. By permission of the publisher, Frederick Warne & Co., Inc.

Illustration of "Humpty Dumpty," from *The Real Mother Goose*, illustrated by Blanche Fisher Wright. Copyright 1916, 1944 by Rand McNally & Company.

"Hoppity," from the book *When We Were Very Young* by A. A. Milne, illustrated by Ernest H. Shepard. Copyright, 1924, by E. P. Dutton & Co., Inc. Renewal, 1952, by A. A. Milne. Reprinted by permission of the publishers.

A Tree Is Nice by Janice May Udry, pictures by Marc Simont. Text copyright © 1956 by Janice Udry. Pictures copyright © 1956 by Marc Simont. Reprinted with permission of Harper & Row, Publishers.

"Clouds," reprinted by permission of G. P. Putnam's Sons from *All Together* by Dorothy Aldis. Copyright 1925, 1926, 1927, 1928, 1934, 1939, 1952 by Dorothy Aldis.

"Spring Rain," from the book *Around and About* by Marchette Chute. Copyright ©, 1957 by E. P. Dutton & Co., Inc., and reprinted by permission of the publishers.

"One Was Johnny," from *The Nutshell Library* by Maurice Sendak. Copyright © 1962 by Maurice Sendak. Reprinted with permission of Harper & Row, Publishers.

Illustrators

Dave Broad: "Who Likes the Rain?"

Ray Der: "Clouds," "Spring Rain"

Ed Tabor: "The Little Red Hen and the Grain of Wheat"

Earl Thollander: "Tommy"

Wendy Wheeler: "Firefly," "The Little Elfman," "Star Light, Star Bright"

Contents

8

Hey Diddle Diddle

Hey, diddle, diddle,
The Cat and the Fiddle,

The Cow jumped over the Moon.

The little Dog laughed
to see such fun,

And the Dish ran away
    with the Spoon.

Sharing Time

1. Why did the little dog laugh?

2. Where do you think the dish
   and the spoon went?

3. What part do you think
   is the funniest?

4. What does fiddle music
   make you want to do?

Who Likes the Rain?

Clara Doty Bates

"I," said the duck, "I call it fun,
For I have my little red rubbers on;
They make a cunning three-toed track
In the soft, cool mud. Quack! Quack! Quack!"

14

Firefly

Elizabeth Madox Roberts

A little light is going by,
Is going up to see the sky,
A little light with wings.

I never could have thought of it,
To have a little bug all lit
And made to go on wings.

15

One Is Good but Two Are Better

Louis Slobodkin

One is good,
But two are better,

You need two people
For a letter.

One pulling a wagon
Is not enough,
You need two
When the road is rough.

One can swing
Alone in the sun,
But you need two
To have more fun.

One in a boat,
Playing down at the shore
Can't go very far
With only one oar,

But if there are two,
Two oars and two friends,
You can row
'Round the world
Before the day ends.

One with a ball
Needs one with a bat;
Baseball is better
Played like that.

One can run,
Or one can lag,
But you need two
For playing tag.

One may hide,
Or one may peek,
But you need two
For hide-and-seek.

Yes, one is good,
But when there are more,
Say two or three
Or more than four,

You all can sing,
And you all can play,
And you all can have
A wonderful day.

26

Sharing Time

1. What can *two* children do?
   Draw pictures to show.

2. What are some of the
   sound-alike words?

3. What is the story
   trying to tell you?

Tommy

Gwendolyn Brooks

I put a seed into the ground
And said, "I'll watch it grow."
I watered it and cared for it
As well as I could know.

One day I walked in my back yard,
And oh, what did I see!
My seed had popped itself right out,
Without consulting me.

The Little Red Hen
and the Grain of Wheat

Retold by Veronica S. Hutchinson

One day the Little Red Hen
was scratching in the farmyard
when she found a grain of wheat.

"Who will plant the wheat?"
said she.

"Not I," said the duck.

"Not I," said the cat.

"Not I," said the dog.

"Very well then,"
said the Little Red Hen,
"I will."

So she planted the grain
of wheat.

After some time the wheat
grew tall and ripe.

"Who will cut the wheat?"
asked the Little Red Hen.

"Not I," said the duck.

"Not I," said the cat.

"Not I," said the dog.

"Very well then, I will,"
said the Little Red Hen.

So she cut the wheat.

"Now," she said,
"who will thresh the wheat?"

"Not I," said the duck.

"Not I," said the cat.

"Not I," said the dog.

"Very well then, I will,"
said the Little Red Hen.

So she threshed the wheat.

When the wheat
was threshed, she said,
"Who will take the wheat
to the mill
to have it ground into flour?"

"Not I," said the duck.

"Not I," said the cat.

"Not I," said the dog.

"Very well then, I will,"
said the Little Red Hen.

So she took the wheat
to the mill.

When the wheat was ground
into flour, she said,
"Who will make this flour
into bread?"

40

"Not I," said the duck.

"Not I," said the cat.

"Not I," said the dog.

"Very well then, I will,"
said the Little Red Hen,
and she baked
a lovely loaf of bread.

Then she said,
"Who will eat the bread?"

42

"Oh! I will," said the duck

"Oh! I will," said the cat.

"Oh! I will," said the dog.

"Oh, no, you won't!"
said the Little Red Hen.
"I will."

And she called her chicks
and shared the bread with them.

Sharing Time

1. What did the Little Red Hen do
   to get the bread?

2. Why didn't the Little Red Hen
   give any bread
   to the duck, cat, or dog?

3. How do you know the Little Red
   Hen was a good mother?

Jack and Jill

Jack and Jill
Went up the hill,
To fetch a pail of water;
Jack fell down
And broke his crown,
And Jill came tumbling after.

Humpty Dumpty

Humpty Dumpty sat on a wall,
Humpty Dumpty had a great fall;
All the King's horses and all the King's men
Couldn't put Humpty Dumpty together again.

The Little Elfman

John Kendrick Bangs

I met a little Elfman once,
　　Down where the lilies blow.
I asked him why he was so small,
　　And why he didn't grow.

He slightly frowned, and with his eye
　　He looked me through and through—
"I'm just as big for me," said he,
　　"As you are big for you!"

48

Hoppity

A. A. Milne

Christopher Robin goes
Hoppity, hoppity,
Hoppity, hoppity, hop.
Whenever I tell him
Politely to stop it, he
Says he can't possibly stop.

If he stopped hopping, he couldn't
   go anywhere,
Poor little Christopher
Couldn't go anywhere . . .
That's why he *always* goes
Hoppity, hoppity,
Hoppity,
Hoppity,
Hop.

A Tree Is Nice

Janice May Udry

Trees are very nice.
They fill up the sky.
They go beside the rivers
and down the valleys.
They live up on the hills.
Trees make the woods.

50

They make everything
beautiful.
    Even if you have
just one tree,
it is nice too.

A tree is nice
because it has leaves.
The leaves whisper
in the breeze
all summer long.

In the fall, the leaves
come down and we play in them.

We walk in the leaves
and roll in the leaves.

We build playhouses
out of the leaves.

Then we pile them up
with our rakes
and have a bonfire.

A tree is nice because
it has a trunk and limbs.
We can climb the tree
and see over all the yards.
We can sit on a limb
and think about things.

54

Or play pirate ship
up in the tree.
If it is an apple tree
we can climb it
to pick the apples.

Cats get away from dogs
by going up the tree.

Birds build nests in trees
and live there.

Sticks come
off the trees too.

We draw in the sand
with the sticks.

56

A tree is nice
to hang a swing in.
    Or a basket of flowers.
    It is a good place to lean
your hoe while you rest.

A tree is nice
because it makes shade.
The cows lie down
in the shade when it is hot.

People have picnics
there too.
And the baby takes his nap
in his buggy in the shade.

A tree is nice
for a house to be near.
The tree shades the house
and keeps it cool.
The tree holds off the wind
and keeps the wind from blowing
the roof off the house sometimes.

60

A tree is nice to plant.

You dig the biggest hole
you can and put the little
tree in.

Then you pour in lots
of water and then the dirt.

You hang the shovel
back in the garage.

Every day for years and YEARS
you watch the little tree grow.
 You say to people,
"I planted that tree."
 They wish they had one
so they go home
and plant a tree too.

62

Sharing Time

1. How do the children have fun with the trees?

2. How does a tree help people and animals?

3. How would you plant a tree?

4. Why do you think a tree is nice?

Clouds

Dorothy Aldis

If I had a spoon
As tall as the sky
I'd dish out the clouds
That go slip-sliding by.

I'd take them right in
And give them to cook
And see if they tasted
As good as they look.

Spring Rain

Marchette Chute

The storm came up so very quick
   It couldn't have been quicker.
I should have brought my hat along,
   I should have brought my slicker.

My hair is wet, my feet are wet,
   I couldn't be much wetter.
I fell into a river once
   But this is even better.

One Was Johnny

Maurice Sendak

1 was Johnny who
lived by himself

2 was a rat who
jumped on his shelf

67

3 was a cat who
chased the rat

4 was a dog who
came in and sat

5 was a turtle who
bit the dog's tail

6 was a monkey who
brought in the mail

7 a blackbird pecked
poor Johnny's nose

8 was a tiger out
selling old clothes

9 was a robber who
took an old shoe

10 was a puzzle.
What should Johnny do?

He stood
on a chair
and said,
"Here's what I'll do—
I'll start
to count backwards

and when
I am through—
if this house
isn't empty
I'll eat
all of you!!!!"

9 was the robber who
left looking pale

8 was the tiger who
chased him to jail

7 the blackbird flew
off to Havana

6 was the monkey who
stole a banana

5 was the turtle who
crawled off to bed

4 was the dog who
slid home on a sled

3 was the cat who
pounced on the rat

2 was the rat who
left with the cat

1 was Johnny who
lived by himself

AND LIKED IT LIKE THAT!

Sharing Time

1. Who came to Johnny's house?

2. What was the funniest thing
   that happened?

3. How did Johnny feel
   when his house was full?

4. How was Johnny clever?

5. If all the animals came
   to *your* house, what
   would you do?

Star Light, Star Bright

Star light, star bright,
The first star I see tonight,
I wish I may, I wish I might
Have the wish I wish tonight.